Wake Up,
ANNIE
MATHER

MIKE DORSEY

This book is a work of nonfiction. Some names and identifying details of people described in this book have been altered to protect their privacy.

ISBN: 978-1-954614-62-8

Dorsey. Mike.
Wake Up, Annie Mather

Edited by: Melisssa Long

Published by Warren Publishing
Charlotte, NC
www.warrenpublishing.net
Printed in the United States

Dedication

To every mother who is devoted to rearing their children—yesterday, today, and tomorrow—may they be cherished for eternity.

CHAPTER 1
WAKE UP, ANNIE MATHER!

My mother, Annie Mather, was buried at the Gate of Heaven cemetery after she died on March 4, 2007. The cemetery is located at the intersection of Georgia and Connecticut Avenues, where engines roar. As a deaf person with hearing aids, I am always amazed when I am inside the cemetery. The rumbling of the cars is somehow silenced, and there is a special kind of quiet resting in the midst of many graves, as if they are books at a library where loud sound is forbidden. I often see a number of visitors sitting on the grass with their beloved, and I imagine they are reading memories that took place in their lives in the absolute stillness and grace of the cemetery.

My father, William Guy, has been buried in this cemetery since January 3, 1974. When I got my driver's license, I would visit Dad often and joke with him.

"Hey, Dad, may I borrow five bucks?"

Dad was thirty-two when he lost his battle with Hodgkin's disease, a cancer of the lymph nodes. Mom was widowed at thirty-one and became a single mother of four little brats: David (age seven), Hannah (six), Emily (five), and me (four). Because Mom knew we were too young to remember Dad, she took every chance she had to talk about him in order to keep him alive for us. Her gift of storytelling made us all feel closer to him. Mom even joked with me from time to time about how we both were four years old when our fathers died. She would say, "Michael, my mother was four when her father died, my twin sister and I were four, and you were four. Do yourself a favor: skip your child's fourth birthday."

For almost four decades, Mom would repeatedly tell us her fondest memories of him. "Your father always wanted his meals simple and edible. For lunch, I usually made him peanut butter and jelly on a toasted English muffin. He'd lick his fingers that were covered with the melted goo of peanut butter and jelly and ask me, 'May I have some more?' If your father did not like the dinner I made him, he would just smile and say, 'Can we *not* have this again?' "

She loved to tell us their funny stories. "Your dad was such a flirt. He would stare and whistle at a woman while I was right there next to him. There was one time when she turned around, and it turned out *she* was a man with long hair. I laughed so hard." Mom didn't like the flirting, but she loved that karma bit him in the ass that time!

Yet, she shared the sad memories as well. "Your father tried to work after his cancer had gotten bad. He was a salesperson for Scribner's Publishing. He would kid with people, saying, 'Please buy from me. I am dying with cancer. Look at the picture of my wife and kids.' "

When Mom was buried, it broke my heart to see her grave so far away from Dad. I did not know she bought that distant plot until the day of her funeral. I am still perplexed by it and wish she had either bought the plot next to my dad or been cremated so her ashes could have been spread on his grave to show some kind of reunion. Being apart thirty-three years, I suppose Mom might have felt it unnecessary to be buried next to him, for she had been alone for so long. Instead, Mom chose to be buried alone, away from all of her family. She also could have opted for cremation to be in the wind with her sister and mother. Her twin, Mimi, had her ashes spread at her favorite places—the beach and next to the farmhouse she adored for decades. I knew Mom was struggling with depression, but she just plopped herself into a hole as if she gave up on life. It was heartbreaking. When my sisters found out the cousins spread Aunt Mimi's ashes at the beach, they were hurt that they were not included. But I think the real hurt was that Mom did not want her remains spread anywhere. Then again, I do not know the full story of why Mom bought her grave site at such a place of isolation. It was as if she never changed, even in eternity, for she was isolated in life.

It's still so strange that I know exactly where Dad's grave is, but it is not so easy for me to find my mom's. I had moved out of state for a job before Mom died, so the visits to her grave site were not as frequent as I would have liked. It is sort of ironic, considering I knew Mom better than I knew Dad.

I hate it when I trample over other people's graves while trying to find her, especially when the weather is hot and my two kids are complaining because they want to get back in the car and turn on the air conditioner. It was simpler visiting

Dad's grave site, especially when I was a bachelor. In addition to being deaf, I also have cerebral palsy. I am unsteady at times as I walk through the hilly landscape—because of the cerebral palsy—and I get self-conscious of what others think of me, especially when it may appear that I cannot handle my alcohol. When I am stepping on the other graves, looking for Mom's, I am sure the ghosts are looking up at me and yelling, "Get off my yard, you drunken bum!"

When I finally find Mom's grave, I usually become speechless because I honestly do not know what to say to a headstone. I was so used to seeing her in person. With Dad, I knew him as a grave and grew comfortable talking to a stone with his name engraved on it—*William Guy Dorsey 1941–1974*. But with Mom, she was a person to me, and talking to her as a grave with her name on the stone—*Anne Mather Dorsey 1942–2007*—was foreign to me. It was as if she resurrected into a rock. I feel funny talking to a stone that was once a person I knew, a person I could see, hug, appreciate, and love. I want to look at Mom and say to her, just like Jesus said to Lazarus, "Wake up, Annie Mather!"

If I could hear Mom talk back to me, she would say, after listening to my dramatic exclamation, "Michael, shut up and get a job!"

Well, I am not Jesus. I will, however, make a sculpture of Mom in the form of this book so people can know how great of a woman she was when she roamed the earth as one of the greatest mothers anyone could have.

᳗

CHAPTER 2
HOOKY

My mom's real name was Anne, and I am not sure how her nickname, Annie, came about. I am just glad it did. Annie encapsulated her and her charming personality. She was not a snobbish, proper Anne, but a down-to-earth cherub. And, boy, did she have the gift of gab. She had wonderful facial expressions and the ability to change her voice in each of the stories she told, especially when impersonating someone who was drunk.

"Oh my gosh, Michael, your first-grade teacher would call me late at night and she would slur, 'Hellooo, Mrs. Dorsheeey? How arrrrre yooou?' " I was amazed because Mom patiently listened to the teacher's incoherent rants for an hour every time she called.

Mom imitating her mother was also very cute. Nana, who was homebound due to having mild dementia, spoke in a high-class and avid-reader manner. "Michael, your Nana was funny today. When I asked how she was doing, she responded, 'Well, Annie, I have been reduced to watching squirrels.' " Mom mimicked Nana's voice and mannerisms to perfection.

Personality aside, Mom was also a delight to look at. She was naturally beautiful and rarely wore makeup. Her rosy cheeks, charismatic smile, wild brown curls, and bright blue eyes—as if they were plucked from the Caribbean—were capable of enchanting anyone in her presence. I have always been envious of her teeth, for they were perfectly aligned while I had a gap between my front two teeth for the longest time. I could not help but sometimes feel like a horse, and I would come up with a corny joke, telling people I owned the Gap.

Mom had one sibling when she was growing up, her identical twin. Aunt Mimi, whose real name was Mary, became Mimi because of Mom. When they were young children, Mom pointed to Aunt Mimi while they were both looking at a mirror in their shared bedroom and said, "Me." Then she pointed to herself and said, "Me." And that was that.

I often could not tell the two of them apart when I was a child because I was too short to see their faces. For instance, when I whined or was simply seeking attention—I was the youngest *and* the brattiest—I would grab Mom's leg. I would then be startled when Aunt Mimi yelled, "Get off of me! I am not your mother."

While their mother, my Nana, was working at the Bethesda Naval Hospital as a psychiatric social worker, her mother, Granny, would stay home and watch the girls to make sure they were on their best behavior. Granny's parents were from Ireland and devout Catholics, so she walked around the house with a rosary in her hand and mumbled to herself, saying prayers and nodding her head with quiet whispers of Jesus, Mary, and Joseph. Some mornings, Mom and Aunt Mimi would skip the bus and run around the house to the backyard where there was nothing but woods, railroad tracks, and more woods. The twins would stop in the yard and look up at Granny as she stood in the living room, looking down at them through the window. They would wave at her to confirm they were okay before disappearing. They would play in the woods all day, stretching out their imaginations and pretending they were in an enchanted forest and talking with tree fairies.

I do not think they ever got into trouble for playing hooky. Honestly, as far as I know, they never got in trouble for anything. It seemed as if Granny did not dare tell Nana what the twins were up to because she did not want to worry Nana. As long as the twins were safe, sound, and home when Nana returned from work, everything was fine. Of course, I never got to meet Granny, so I do not know for certain.

Growing up, the twins were always catching people's attention whenever they were in public. And they loved it. Nana made sure their clothes were not only alike, but also impeccable, which made the twins a pleasant sight for all who passed by them. At school, the twins were popular because they were identical and attractive. Besides wearing nice clothes, their bright blue eyes, long eyelashes, pretty smiles, and curly brown hair helped make them stand out in the crowds.

Their school, Stone Ridge, was a private, all-girls Catholic school situated off of Wisconsin Avenue in Bethesda,

Maryland. Nana, who also attended that school when she was the twins' age, would drop off the girls at school on her way to work at the hospital, which was practically down the street from the school.

Mom surprised me once when she told me how her fights with Aunt Mimi were sometimes violent when they were stuck at home as kids. Once, they chased each other with pencils. Why did they fight? I don't know. Why don't I know? I did not ask. As a little boy, I loved to just sit on the stool and listen to Mom tell me stories about her childhood and what happened thereafter. It never occurred to me to interrupt her. Now, looking back, I could have gotten secondhand lung cancer from Mom's chain-smoking addiction, inhaling all of those toxic clouds. My eyes, fortunately, did not get blinded by the burning nicotine, though at times it felt like they were on fire.

When I say I loved listening to mom's stories, I really mean I was actively trying to read her lips. It takes a lot of concentration to figure out what words are forming as they come out of someone's mouth. I have to be absolutely still so I can process each word carefully to make sure I understand everything clearly. I think I became comfortable not asking questions because I find it mentally exhausting to watch a mouth move like a bingo machine as I wait for the number—or, in this case, a word—to be spit out. I never felt too exhausted when Mom talked to me, though. I was always so engrossed by what she had to say. Honestly, now that Mom is not alive, I do wish I had asked about her childhood adventures.

***

Recently, my sister found a newspaper article that featured a picture of the twins as teenagers while they were attending Stone Ridge, and I scanned a copy. They were cute as they sat in their seats, reading books that were placed in front of them. When I posted the picture of Mom and Aunt Mimi on Facebook without giving away who was who, a friend of mine commented that the young woman on the right was definitely my mom for she looked confident. I corrected her and thought it was sad that my friend thought Mom did not look confident. Of course, I did not ask her why. I just let the emotions twirl around me as if my friend had seen Mom as a butterfly with broken wings struggling to flutter with the wind. I realized later why one might think, at first, that Mom was being rather bashful since she smiled with her lips softly closed. Aunt Mimi smiled with her mouth slightly open, as if she were about to shout.

Somehow, I was taken back to a memory that often visits me. Mom was walking to mass in a blizzard, with strong winds blowing in her face and snow covering her tracks as if saying her existence was not something to notice or remember. Mom's words would then echo within my soul: "My mother once looked at me as I was vacuuming her house while Mimi was out working as an editor and asked me, 'Why can't you get a job like Mimi?' " Nana always praised Aunt Mimi for wanting to be an editor, a position she thought Mom should also pursue. To Nana, anything was better than being a housewife.

Though Mom and Aunt Mimi were identical, and they had married brothers, our families were incredibly different. And I hated how different we were. I used to look at pictures of my double-first cousins with envy. Unlike us, they would be dressed in immaculate clothes, and their oldest brother would be smiling, looking completely normal. Pictures of our mothers together also made me sad, as I saw Mom in her discount T-shirt and jeans and Aunt Mimi in a fancy shirt with dress pants.

I know I am a bit of a drama king, and I'm aware that I think too often in black and white, so I know I am wrong to believe that Aunt Mimi was the better twin, the fortunate one—that Mom was the lesser twin—but I cannot help it. My view has been distorted with envy and embarrassment since I was from the "lesser" mother who gave birth to me, a "lesser" son with disabilities.

My mom and aunt both had their troubles, however. It was not until many years later that I learned they suffered similar afflictions, which led them to similarly tragic deaths. They were living very different lives, but they both battled depression and were addicted to nicotine, which caused them both to die in their early sixties, about two years apart, from lung cancer.

It is really sad to see the pictures of those two beautiful young ladies in great health, knowing they died such ugly deaths. Aunt Mimi could barely walk on her own, and she often wore a bandana to cover her loss of hair from chemotherapy. Mom's last days were just as bad as she struggled to walk. Once, she fell and cracked her ribs. And the cancer didn't just affect her physically. Mom became confused mentally. Sometimes, she'd restlessly wander at night because she didn't realize what time it was.

I feel like I have to remind myself that both women had suffered. Aunt Mimi was never the better half because she remained married and had three perfect children and money. Mom was never the lesser half because she was widowed, had four children (two with disabilities), and was poor. They both had grandchildren, but those relationships were severed too soon due to their nicotine addictions.

My siblings and double-first cousins share a similar pain, which is never openly talked about between us. We know, deep inside, that our mothers would still be alive if not for their addictions. To think, their mother puffed her cigarettes instead of inhaling the smoke and lived until she was eighty-nine. The twins would have been seventy-nine today, getting ready to celebrate their eightieth birthdays next March, if they had done the same thing.

Even still, addiction is a disease. That is what I learned during my own road to recovery from smoking and drinking. The solution that works to help conquer addiction has to come from within. You have to be willing to acknowledge that you have a problem and need help. My double-first cousins and my siblings might have had different lives, but we all felt the same powerlessness as we watched our mothers transform from beautiful roses to dried petals before they faded away.

꒰꒱

CHAPTER 3
THE REAL LITTLE WOMEN

Often, Mom would tell me how much she valued the memory of eating dinner as a family with Nana, Aunt Mimi, and Granny.

"It was the only time in the day when all four of us were together," she told me. "It felt like we were characters right out of the book *Little Women*. My mom's father, Max, died when she was four, and my dad died when I was four, just like you, Mikey. He died in his sleep from a rare skin disease." (To this day, I do not recall what it was exactly. Why? Because like an idiot, I did not ask.) "Your nana and I shared the pain of knowing how hard life was growing up without a father, though we rarely talked about it. We sort of knew in our hearts, and I felt we did not need to bring up the topic of being fatherless as long as we had each other. Being without a dad brought us all closer together."

I think, however, there was a difference in how Mom and Aunt Mimi coped with growing up without their father, Max. Mom wanted to bond with a parent like her sister had, and since Max was gone, there was a splinter in her heart. Although Mom never said it in words, I felt her sadness by looking at her facial expressions. Reading the lips of a person who's saying they're fine when their eyes and mouth droop in silence ... well, that speaks volumes. I witnessed Mom's heartache every time she told me a story of growing up feeling left out. She always thought she was lagging behind as Nana and Aunt Mimi discussed the latest read or had a light tiff over which ingredients to use to cook dinner. They shared common interests in reading and cooking, whereas Mom always wanted to do something outdoorsy. As they discussed in depth what words to use in *The New York Times* crossword puzzle, Mom would be bored and want to do something else, like go for a walk. There was a picture of Mom sitting on her father's lap while outside, and I could see they both shared a common interest in being out in the fresh air. Both Mom and Max looked serene, as if they were molded for the outdoors.

Fortunately for Mom, the four ladies used to take summer vacations to the Delaware shore, where they all felt like they were in heaven with the smell of saltwater in the air and the sun warming their faces as they sat on the beach. When all the little women were at the beach, negative thoughts were not in existence, especially with the ocean breeze kissing their cheeks and cooling them down from the hot sun. Aunt Mimi and Mom were a pair again as they swam side by side together, floating on their backs in the ocean beyond the waves so they could hear each other talk. Their toes could be seen above the water, as if they were tiny turtle heads poking out each time the current shifted.

Mom and Aunt Mimi both pleaded with Nana to buy a cottage by the ocean, but Nana was frugal with money—righteously so, as she lived through the Great Depression. Nana thought it was better to leave her money in stocks and mutual funds. Our family has always been money conscious. Granny's brother, Ed Mahoney, looked after Granny when her husband died. Great-Uncle Ed had been fortunate with his dollars and cents. He made sure his widowed sister was taken care of while she was rearing Nana as a single parent. Then when Nana became a widow and single parent herself, Granny took her turn in helping Nana with her finances and watching the twins the best she could. When Dad died, the cycle continued. Nana assisted Mom in getting her bills paid so she could have food, heat, water, and electricity for her four children.

In the years leading up to Nana's death, although Granny was not around in person, I could sense her presence when Mom, Aunt Mimi, and Nana got together once a year at Bethany Beach, Delaware, for summer vacation. There is a picture of Nana, Aunt Mimi, and Mom on the porch of a cottage. It was taken probably thirty years ago. It was considered a Hallmark photo as it was rare for the three of them to be together since Aunt Mimi had moved out of state to be with her husband, whose work required him to travel. Nana sat up to pose for the picture while taking a break from reading the *New York Times* and *Washington Post*, her lit cigarette resting on the ashtray. She wore a white beach hat to keep her hair still from the ocean breeze that came up from the south. As it was cool that evening, even with the sun still shining, Nana had put on a cashmere sweater, the soft color of maize, and white slacks. Aunt Mimi wore a white, button-down sweater with a black T-shirt, probably from Ann Taylor, since all the clothes she handed down to my mom had the Ann Taylor label. Mom also wore a white sweater, but I am not sure who made it. Most of her clothes were generic sweatshirts, jeans, and T-shirts. All three women said they loved that picture, and so did my cousins, my siblings, and I. Many of us still consider Bethany Beach a special place, especially now that all three women are with Granny in spirit. Perhaps they're walking on the sand together, leaving footprints as reminders of what is truly important: family.

***

The three women were the anchors keeping the family together. They were the ones who brought us all together at least once a year for Thanksgiving and/or Christmas.

On many Thanksgiving holidays, Mom, my siblings, and I went to Aunt Mimi's husband, Uncle Mike's, farm in the boondocks of the West Virginia mountains. The scenery was perfect for a Thanksgiving celebration, as the property was over five hundred acres of open fields and mountains. For about the first twenty years of my life, Uncle Mike had just one farmhouse on the fields near the foothills. It was next to a long, windy, and bumpy driveway, which was a one-way road that stretched far beyond Uncle Mike's property. We occasionally walked to meet his neighbors, the Hipps, who lived deep in the woods in a small house with a front porch. Mr. Hipp barely had any teeth. The same went for Mrs. Hipp, as her teeth had gone missing too. Mr. Hipp was slim while Mrs. Hipp was slightly overweight. I never thought of the couple as too hillbilly or hideous to mingle with. I liked them. They were kind to me. More kindness was in their souls than in Uncle Mike's.

Uncle Mike may have been mean toward me, but I can sympathize a bit since he had it rough with losing both of his brothers, one of whom was my father. They were his best friends. I was spoiled, and Uncle Mike was not pleased with me acting like a brat while looking like Dad. Dad had been tough and fierce when he was alive. As for me, I would hide behind Mom's legs for security to keep myself away from Uncle Mike's angry eyes piercing through me. I am sure if Dad had been alive, I would not have been so spoiled. He would have taught me how to man up somehow, and then maybe Uncle Mike would have liked me better. As a kid, I did not have the ability to be psychoanalytical about why our relationships were dysfunctional. I was only able to decipher who was good and who was bad based on how I was treated. Mr. Hipp would be in the "good" category; Uncle Mike was in the "bad."

For everyone else at the farm, it seemed like a great idea for the families to get together. The cousins and my siblings found friendships among one another. Mom had Aunt Mimi. My siblings—David, Hannah, and Emily—all had gotten along well with our cousins—John, Meg, and Paul.

God, even their names sound perfect.

David and John were close in age; Emily and Meg were the same age; and although Hannah and John were the same age, Hannah paired up well with Paul. It would have been supercool if the two leftover Mikeys, Uncle Mike and me, could have been friends.

Even though I wanted to be treated as an equal among my cousins, Uncle Mike would not allow it. One of the random events we did at the farm for Thanksgiving was shoot empty aluminum cans off a branch with rifles. I felt so much resentment and envy as I watched Paul being treated like a man when he was a year younger than me simply because he had easy access to the rifles his dad trusted him with. I had to stand by and watch the young boys shoot cans with their guns and inflate their egos. Moments like those made me wish I did not have any disabilities so I would not be considered a freak and would be allowed to play with guns.

Although David has an intellectual disability, Uncle Mike seemed to respect him only because his brother, Uncle Joey, also is intellectually disabled. Now that I look back, I honestly can say that I don't blame Uncle Mike for having trouble respecting me when I was a whiner who found Mommy whenever things went wrong. Even my sisters did not want me to come with them when I tried to join them on a hike. I felt rejected and oversensitive. Therefore, I cried like a baby. Uncle Mike would then approach me with his children and my sisters behind and ask me what was wrong. Like a brat who did not know how to voice his feelings, I just shrugged my shoulders and walked away so I could sink further into my (somewhat) self-made misery. I guess there should have been a manual somewhere in school for students to learn how to understand the difference between misery by choice and misery by default.

As a kid, I remember the excitement I felt riding in Mom's Volkswagen Beetle as she drove down the bumpy, windy, and long driveway to Uncle Mike's little farmhouse. I always kept an eye out for the marker that stated we were at the farm as we entered through the trees on the country road. Uncle Mike had a big, green sign with white, cursive letters that spelled out, John & Meg's Farm. It didn't dawn on me until years later, perhaps when I was in my late teens, that Paul's name was not on the sign. It was made shortly after Uncle Mike had bought the property and remained unchanged even after Paul was born. I did not bother asking anyone why that was.

I feel sad when I think about how Dad spent time at the farm soon after Uncle Mike bought the property. I am not sure what they did there, but I imagine he shot a few rounds with his rifle. I did not ask, of course, for any details when Mom used to tell me about Dad visiting the farm. It was not often that Dad could visit because it was around the same time he got sick.

The little farm was neat, and Aunt Mimi was so hospitable. She always provided me with a can of Mountain Dew, my favorite soda. The farmhouse had real, handmade hardwood floors. There was a small living room, full bath, master bedroom, kitchen, and dining room all on one floor. The second floor had two bedrooms. I remember seeing flies stuck between the window glass and the screen in the room that I slept in. Some were dead, and some were alive. When I looked outside the window, I would see nothing but mountains in the distance, the country road, and a creek that went along the side of the property, which paralleled the road. In the living room, we mostly hung out and watched television if the antenna was able to connect to a show like football. Without cable, the TV was usually hopeless, so we played games instead. Some moments were good at the farm, especially since we had lots of free drinks and food.

The farmhouse was remodeled over the years, but the structure remained intact. The original house had an old deck with some holes I almost fell through on more than one occasion. There was a little roof over the deck to keep us dry and cool when we sat outside. Since the farmhouse was just steps away from the country road, there used to be the occasional passerby in the night. We would see their headlights shine brightly as the car neared the farmhouse, and with my hearing aids, even I was able to hear the tires on the gravel. As it was otherwise silent and dark in the night, Paul would take a flashlight and shine it at the fields to show me the many pairs of bright eyes looking straight at us. They belonged to all the deer that lived out there. It was amazing to see so many of them. As kids, Paul and I would go up to the deer that had been shot and were dying in the fields. We had a selfless and sincere bonding moment where our egos were put aside and we were just two friends completely focused on the frightened immobile deer. We gave the deer nuts and some vegetables, hoping she would eat and revive. The next visit, we mourned for the deer whose life had been taken away too soon.

Although some memories of being at the farm for Thanksgiving were bitter, there were others that were sweet. My brain tends to automatically focus on the bitter moments, and it is up to me to manually diverge my thought process to what is good and balance it with the bad. After all, there is both good and bad everywhere in life. It is ludicrous to be one-sided since nothing is all good or all bad.

Sometimes, I even asked Uncle Mike if I could stay at his farmhouse. It had been less frequented with visitors after he had another house built farther away from the country road on top of a foothill on the mountain. The new driveway was insanely steep; it scared me every time I drove on it. I had to decide when it would be a good time to shift the gear to second or first as I nervously gripped the steering wheel with both hands, hoping to God I would not drive off the road and end up in a ditch.

Each time I called Uncle Mike to ask if I could stay at his original farmhouse, I would quiver with fear. I was afraid he would say no, and I also felt bad for calling him only to ask if I could use his farm when I would not have called otherwise. If I had tried to call him just to chat, I imagine he would have said something like, "Hey, Mike, how are you doing? Still being a stay-at-home bum and bothering your mother?"

Just kidding.

Not really.

I would have loved it and felt more enthusiastic about calling him if I knew he was going to say something like, "Hey, Mike! Let's get together soon. I want to hear about how you are doing."

Maybe, deep inside, he wanted to tell me to grow up, get a job, and leave Mom alone. I did not realize I was living off Mom because I was struggling to find a career I could succeed in. I wanted to do stand-up comedy, and I was trying to make my daytime job as a social worker work out. However, the comedy business is very hard to succeed in—especially for me, thanks to my speech impediment and cerebral palsy—and social work is toxic, so it was disheartening for me to still be living with Mom at age thirty-five. It would have been awesome if I had succeeded in comedy. That way, I probably would not have been the black sheep anymore and could have left Mom alone. I also could have given her a nicer home to live in. I just wanted to make Mom smile. It was not as though I had deliberately said to myself, "I am going to destroy Mom's life by falling off the career ladder over and over again." Unfortunately, I did not realize how much my struggles affected Mom since she did not say a word to me until she was close to her deathbed.

Uncle Mike would have had every right to tell me how much of a pain I was being for everyone, especially Mom. However, instead of lecturing me, he simply let me hang out at his farmhouse. Having access to the farmhouse gave me a break from feeling anxious and depressed. But I often realize too late that, no matter where I go, I will struggle with reality until I learn how to face it.

When I went to hang out at the farmhouse alone, it was exciting at first because I did not have to worry about ego-tripping with the cousins or being afraid of Uncle Mike getting mad at me for whatever reason. Although it is hard to admit, I often wished Dad was the one who owned the property instead of Uncle Mike. It would have been awesome if we'd had our own sign out front that read, David & Hannah's farm. Who cares if Emily's name or mine was not on it? The property would have been ours, and we would have been welcoming to our guests instead of bowing to our hosts.

With the drama aside, I have to say, I really did like the farmhouse. Everything in it was simple and charming. There was a wonderfully old wooden stove in the living room, which was the main heat source. Since the house was tiny, the stove had no problem with keeping the rooms warm and cozy. In the kitchen, there was an old refrigerator that was like the one Mom had in her kitchen—a long, stainless steel handle that you pulled to open and close the door. The wooden stove across from the fridge was absolutely hands-off, as Uncle Mike had made it loud and clear for everyone to not touch it or else. He and Aunt Mimi were weird about us—usually me—breaking their things. I was often scared to use the toilet in the bathroom because Aunt Mimi kept warning me that I would break it if I did not know what I was doing, which was ridiculous. I mean, all I had to do was turn the handle downward like everyone else, right? Jesus. Mom also believed I would break her appliances if I dared try to cook or clean.

"Mom, I just want to throw my clothes in the wash, put in the right amount of detergent, and then turn the knob to start. That is how you're supposed to wash your clothes, right? You and Aunt Mimi really are twins. Do you honestly think I am going to tackle or smash the toilet just to get it to flush? Do you think I am going to put myself in the washer to give myself a bath?" Good grief.

***

For Christmas, we usually ate our holiday dinner at Nana's house, which was fine with me. I loved visiting her house because I knew I was going to get a check from her. When dinner was over, Nana would hand out Christmas cards to me and all my siblings. Each one had a check inside. The rest of the night, though, was boring because Mom and Nana would talk to each other while I plopped in front of the thirteen-inch television. There was nothing really to watch, and I could not wait to go home where my toys were.

As I grew older, I liked being at Nana's for a different reason. As I started to care more about how I fit into society,

I felt important when I sat inside her nice home. She had marble end tables and Chinese lamps with satin lampshades. I felt reassured that, somehow, I was living a very privileged life. When we returned to Mom's house, I felt a bit sad to see cracked walls and ceilings and a kitchen light that was tinted with burnt tar from cigarette smoke. There was not a Chinese lamp with a satin lampshade or a marble end table anywhere in sight. There was not even any air conditioning.

Nana owned her nice home. Uncle Mike owned his nice mansion, farmhouse, new lodge, and over five hundred acres of land to roam freely on. We were always wearing invisible tags on our clothes that spelled Visiting Misfits.

With Nana, Aunt Mimi, and Mom all passed on, there has not been another family gathering with the double-first cousins. My siblings and I spend our holidays separately with our own families. Perhaps I should try to find a way to have an annual Thanksgiving get together with only my siblings and their families, but, honestly, I like being with just my wife and two children for the holidays. It is much better than pretending to be nice to my siblings. It will take more than one family therapy session to get all the crap out in the open, and for us to finally have a good relationship.

CHAPTER 4

MOTHERS

I really miss living in Bethesda, Maryland. Most of my memories reside there. Each time I drive by the naval hospital, I recall stories of Nana helping veterans there as their psychiatric social worker and her dropping off Mom and Aunt Mimi at Stone Ridge school beforehand. Nana was one of the first members of the Stone Ridge graduating class. One day, as probably the last survivor of her class, Nana accepted the honor of taking part in an event on campus. She was asked to participate in a groundbreaking ceremony for a new building and was pictured in the media posing with a shovel. Mom would smile and shake her head while retelling that story. "I cannot believe Mother, an eighty-something-year-old little homebody, was hoisting a shovel as the guest of honor at such an event!"

Mother was what Mom called Nana. I loved my mom too much to call her that. It sounds so formal. It sounds like a word to use if I was talking about Annie Mather with a stranger. "My mother ..." When I heard Mom refer to Nana as Mother, I felt a little sad inside because I sensed their relationship was somehow estranged. "Mom" is a word that means parent and friend to me. Mom was my parent and my close friend. I miss her terribly.

Whatever the relationship was with my mom and her mother, no one in my family today can doubt Nana's generosity. She poured out money to both her daughters their entire lives. She got them into Stone Ridge, paid their college tuition, and then sent them to Europe as a graduation gift so they could celebrate their four years of hard work. Mom would tell me the story about how she was saved by a local Brit in London when buying a pack of cigarettes, and for whatever reason, it tickled me. She mimicked the local Brit's accent when she recalled how he warned her to not speak "American" at the store when buying smokes to avoid being overcharged. "Instead," he said, "use an accent sounding like mine and ask for a pair of fags." I was too engaged by her storytelling to comprehend that she had sadly been addicted to smoking since she was sixteen. I used to joke that she looked like a dragon puffing out smoke, and I would pat myself on the back for being able to still read her lips while my eyes were burning from the smoke. I would sit there instead, being fascinated by Mom telling me stories about when she was at a bar in college, wearing a Humphrey Bogart brimmed hat, smoking a cigarette, and ordering milk. She thought she was cool. I did too.

I loved the story about when she came back from Europe and was lounging on the front yard of Nana's house with Aunt Mimi, drinking beer and smoking cigarettes. They thought it would be a good idea to send a picture of themselves to Nana. She was in California on her honeymoon since she had married again to a retired doctor, my Poppa, Edward Luongo. The picture infuriated Nana. She called the twins and scolded them. "Girls, you cut that grass and never set foot on the front yard again. My neighbors!"

Nana lived in a prestigious neighborhood where there was an invisible ethics code by which everyone had to abide. Everyone had to act civilized and proper. Shenanigans and tomfoolery were not tolerated or accepted. With the twins sunbathing on the yard, smoking cigarettes, and drinking beer, it was as if a scene was recreated from *Animal House*, where partiers were lounging on campus with booze and cigarettes instead of being well-behaved students who focused on making good grades and being goody two-shoes. Mom and Aunt Mimi were like the partiers, and Nana was like the dean, infuriated and humiliated by the fact that the students dared to bathe in the sun, drink beer, and smoke cigarettes while the grass grew too long compared to the neighbors' freshly cut yards.

As some months went by, Aunt Mimi found a job as an editor, and Mom stayed home to help clean up the inside of the house. Nana seemed pleased with Aunt Mimi and disappointed with Mom since she was still at home. Mom wanted to be a stay-at-home wife and parent, which made Nana lose sleep. Nana was a proud woman, being independent and working full-time with a master's degree in social work, and she wanted that for her daughters. She did not want them to be submissive to men. I felt bad for Mom when she told me the story of Nana being disappointed with her career choice. Each time she told the story to me,

I could see sadness in her eyes when she said, "Michael, I just wanted to be a mother and a wife. It seemed as if I had missed the train on women's rights to work; it was never my calling. Mom was disappointed."

I could imagine Mom in Nana's house, vacuuming the carpet while Aunt Mimi was off at work and Nana shaking her head at her with a snobbish rub of disapproval. When I imagine Mom being given the nose down from Nana, I want to go back in time to give her a great big hug and tell her, "You are going to be the best mother and wife anyone could ask for! I love you!"

Of course, at that time she would have said to me, "Who the hell are you?"

CHAPTER 5
DOUBLE WEDDING

When Aunt Mimi told the family at dinner that she was in a serious relationship with her boyfriend, Mike, Mom knew Aunt Mimi was to be married soon, and it scared her. Mom said to me, "I did not know what to do. I was still single, and the thought of being alone frightened me." Mom always subscribed to the belief that God takes care of the fatherless and widows. Well, God seemed to look after Mom as she struggled with being single while her twin was out and about with a man to marry. One night, Aunt Mimi asked Mom to come with her on a double date. Mike was living with his brother, Bill, who had recently broken up with his girlfriend. Mom decided to go. She said she never laughed so hard as she did with Dad. Apparently, Dad danced like a chicken on the table in the restaurant that night before being asked to leave. Mom said,

"Even the owner chuckled at Dad, saying to him, 'Sorry, pal, but you have to go.' "

One night, after several dates, the brothers went to pick up the twins from Nana's house. Snow was falling hard, so Nana pleaded with everyone to have dinner at her home instead. While Nana was fussing about needing some ingredients from the store to prepare a meal she had in mind, Mom offered to walk to the store, which was about a ten-minute walk, give or take, by the railroad behind Nana's backyard. Dad decided to follow along. As they walked hand in hand on the railroad with the trees and ground covered in snow, I imagine the view of the winter wonderland could not have been more enchanting. Mom said she listened to him talk, she watched the snow melt on his neatly combed hair, and when she looked into his hazel eyes, she knew he was the man to marry.

I am not sure whose idea it was to have a double wedding or how the planning went since Mom did not go into that with me all of the years we sat in the kitchen in our old home. I should not be surprised, for Mom was not good with details, especially when it came to planning an event. It was not her thing. I also have no idea how the wedding came about because I never asked.

I rarely ask questions to investigate what people tell me. I wonder if it is because I am deaf. Even with residual hearing, I miss a lot of what is said as I sit in front of someone and try to read their lips, but I do not bother asking someone who is not deaf to repeat what they are saying. It is a painful norm for non-deaf people, even when they are family, to get frustrated when they are asked to repeat themselves more than once by deaf or hard-of-hearing people. It is like the time when my sister Hannah told me a joke to get us laughing. She ended up crying in frustration after she had to repeat the punch line because I was driving and could not keep my eyes on the road and read her lips at the same time. I then felt bad that I had ruined our chance to have a good time.

After that, I always got jealous when Hannah had more fun with Paul, our double-first cousin who was a year younger than me. I would get mad at both of them for having too much fun, which gave them both more of a reason to not hang out with me. They would get annoyed with me for complaining about not being able to understand what was so funny since I could not hear what they were saying. I only tagged along because I wanted to be with my buddies, especially when we were about to go to a party and get crazy while drinking and smoking pot. With my sister being a college student and in a sorority, there were always parties to attend. I got a fake ID with a picture of a man who looked nothing like me, but as long as I showed the bartender what appeared to be a driver's license, it was good enough. We had to make sure we played it safe so we would not get into trouble or get the bar in trouble for serving alcohol to minors. The three of us liked to drink; I especially liked to mingle. However, when I stood next to Paul, all the ladies wanted to hang out with him because he was handsome. He was taller than me and had a bigger build, plus he could hear and talk like a normal dude. I, on the other hand, could barely be described as a talking dog. I was short, wore mechanical dog ears, and almost barked when I talked due to my speech impediment. I felt like I was Paul's pet as the ladies patted my head but then made out with Paul. Jealousy and beer do not mix well for me.

When we were all hanging out at a bar, the more I drank, the more I sulked and the deeper I sunk into self-pity. I could not score with a woman, and being a dysfunctional drunk did not make me any more popular. No one wanted to be with me, and I fell down a rather disturbing rabbit hole of anger and misery. I was angry at Paul for being normal. I was angry at Hannah for having too much fun with him and believed she wished Paul was her brother since he was normal and fun and I was not.

There was one day in particular when I got really livid at Hannah. We were at her apartment, and in the midst of her party where everyone was having a good time but me because I once again could not hear what was being said and felt left out, she finally turned to me, acknowledging my presence and said, "Turn up the stereo." Like a brat, I said no in front of her friends and Paul. Hannah then came to me and threw a cup of water in my face. Everyone laughed, and the rest of the night was a blur. I vaguely remember going to a convenience store next to the apartment and chewing acid on a piece of paper with Paul before spitting it out at a cereal box where it stuck on Captain Crunch's face.

One night, Paul and Hannah left to go out without telling me. I was upstairs in the bedroom as a guest at Uncle Mike's house for another Christmas gathering, this time in Miami Beach. I went downstairs to look for everyone, and I found that all of my siblings and cousins had left me behind. It was as if I didn't matter to anyone except their dog, Hunter, a beautiful golden Labrador. Hunter was older, calm, and sweet. We kept each other company while everyone else was out. After my siblings and cousins finally arrived back home, they were giggling as they walked by Hunter and me. They said, "Hey, Mike. Hey, Hunter," before disappearing into the kitchen. I looked at Hunter, feeling sad, and said to him, "Hey, Hunter, we are both alike. We are like family dogs, you and me. We get to do tricks to please our humans. If you fetch, roll, and sit at people's commands, they tell you, 'Good boy.' When they tell me to guess what their lips are saying without using voices, they also tell me, 'Good boy.' "

I guess that is why I do not ask questions out loud. I do not want to frustrate anyone and be even more disliked. I just smile when I don't understand and move on as quickly as I can.

Anyway, what I *do* know about the twins marrying the Dorsey brothers is that Uncle Mike and Dad were not well received by Nana. Mom said to me, "Mother warned us to not marry the two brothers because they were from a broken home with unhappy, alcoholic parents who struggled financially because of the drink. She believed we would be happy marrying men who had happier backgrounds and money."

Of course, that seems rather mean at first, and I could call Nana an old hag for talking that way about my father. But I think Nana meant well. She just wanted to make sure her daughters were happy. She couldn't see past Dad and Uncle Mike's background, but Mom and Aunt Mimi could. They tossed aside the money (or lack thereof) and alcoholism as if they were flies in soup and saw the men for who they really were. To them, they were men to love and cherish because they had good hearts and souls. The twins and the brothers were smitten, and no one, not even Nana, could get in the way of their love for each other.

Based on the picture I have of Mom and Dad posing for a photoshoot after their double wedding with Aunt Mimi and Uncle Mike, the weather could not have been better. It was a sunny spring, as the date of their marriage was May 15, 1965. In the Washington, DC, area, which includes Bethesda, spring is by far the most beautiful time of year to visit, especially when people come from all over the world to view the cherry blossom trees that bloom white flowers all throughout the monuments along the Potomac River.

I must say, I find it really incredible how Japan responded to the atomic bomb not by retaliation but by giving away their beloved trees as a truce. Although I am currently living in North Carolina, I have a cherry blossom tree in my backyard along with Japanese maple trees; small paths wind through the garden so I can be closer to home.

Back to the double wedding. As the foursome—Aunt Mimi, Uncle Mike, Dad, and Mom—stepped out of the church as newlyweds, their futures seemed bright; they were going to spend their lives together, raising their children side by side. Cousins would play while the men watched the Redskins and the twins talked about God knows what, for they had their own twin language and codes no one else seemed to decipher. Whenever we visited each other, we tried to get their attention, but it was pointless. They transcended into their own world, as if they entered an enchanted forest and were talking with the tree fairies in tree-fairy language. Therefore, it became customary to just leave the twins alone, which I am sure they loved for their duties as mothers were temporarily lifted for the duration of the visit.

As much as I wish to tell you that the glorious wedding day lasted forever with eternal sunny skies, I cannot. Dark clouds were always brewing nearby. I cannot help but compare Mom's life to Job's when his faith was tested as the devil bargained with God, saying if he made Job's life beyond terrible, he would win Job's soul. I am in no position to believe Mom was also bargaining. I am not God, and I will never fully understand God's ways, but I do believe Mom's faith was tested as she was forced to live through a storm that darkened her beautiful soul for the next forty years.

~

CHAPTER 6
DANDELIONS

I have come to love dandelions. When I grew up, they were all over our yard. Mom told me Dad could not promise her a rose garden, but she was happy with a garden of dandelions. Many people do not like them because they are pesky weeds. To me, they are good reads, like short stories from Hemingway. Dandelions serve their purpose as they attract bees to help beautify the world. They shine brightly with their exquisite, yellow petals. Their scent is precious. Nobody will be sorry to put a dandelion under their nose, for they will find the fragrance most pleasant. Dandelions are kind to children and bring them happiness. Kids pull the flowers out of the ground and give them to their parents as sweet bouquets. Even in their afterlife, the dandelions turn themselves into white seeds so children can blow them to new parts of the earth for more room to bloom. There is such joy in children's eyes as they watch the seeds swim in the spring and summer breezes.

Mom was a lot like a dandelion. Her beauty radiated, she was kind to her children, and in her afterlife, her love still floats like that of a white seed being carried by eternal, gentle winds.

Dad found their house on Greenlawn Drive, with a yard full of dandelions and clovers, shortly after what happened at their apartment in Riverdale, Maryland. A stranger had broken in and entered the bedroom where David and Hannah were sleeping as babies. David was one and Hannah was just a few months old. Mom nudged Dad to wake him up and told him there was a man in their kids' room. In a flash, Dad chased him out of the apartment with his rifle, and Mom heard a shot fired. She thought that was the end of Dad. She believed he was going to jail, but she was relieved when Dad came back disappointed because he missed the son of a bitch. That area is now known as an unsafe neighborhood, so I assume the crime rate was rising when Mom and Dad were still living there. Riverdale is in Prince George's County, which is east of Montgomery County. Montgomery County is considered the safer county to live in now.

When Dad showed Mom the house on Greenlawn Drive, she fell in love with it at first sight, especially when she saw the kitchen. Most kitchens in houses are the centerpieces of family life, and Mom felt this particular room was special. There were two tall, double windows facing south above the sink. The light from the sun was bright and warm, shining through the windows from morning to evening as the sun rose in the east, waded across the southern skies, and set in the west. Dad had decided to look for a house to rent because he received word from his boss at Scribner Publishing that he might be relocating. Mom did not care; she felt at home.

After moving into the house, Mom and Dad thought the outlook seemed promising since they lived closer to Aunt Mimi and Uncle Mike in the same city of Bethesda. Since Dad was the fun guy of the bunch, he often invited Uncle Mike and Aunt Mimi over for get-togethers and birthday parties for the little ones. Mom said the neighbors loved him. Everyone would stop by to say hello and hang out as Dad was so entertaining and welcoming. Mr. Lowe from across the street, who lived there for years after Dad died, said to me once, "I loved your dad." No one dared to mention Dad's cancer. A few months after Dad and Mom had gotten married, Dad went to see the doctor about a lump he felt under his arm. I honestly do not know how Mom felt when she received the terrible news that Dad had cancer. I never found it necessary to ask. I have always been that way, not inquiring too much of another person. The ironic thing about that was I became a social worker, which is a profession of asking questions, though I failed miserably at diving deep into people's lives. What I do know is that everyone, especially Mom, hoped and prayed he would grow old with her.

***

When dandelions die, they first start by raising up their sepals, little lines of green from underneath the yellow flowers, and hugging them so tight that the yellow petals are no longer in sight, as if they were protected from a storm in a shelter. When this happens, the sepals then become brownish green, and it would be easy to mistake the dandelions for dead because the yellow flowers are gone and the brownish green makes the weeds look rather hideous. But the dandelions have one more roar left in them before they finally croak. A few days later, the sepals ease their grips and open up again, only this time, the yellow petals have metamorphosed into white, feathery hairs that are seeds waiting for the wind to carry them into the skies and trusting it to take them wherever they are meant to be.

Dad's sickness was like the sepals coming from underneath him to close him tightly forever. Like the dandelion's resurrection, Dad's life did not stop when he took his last breath. From one dandelion, there are many white, feathery hairs soaring in the skies and bringing new life wherever they land. I like to believe that since my parents both went to church and Dad even went to seek spiritual help from monks when he was sick, they both knew deep inside their hearts that death does not stop life. Life continues forever just like the dandelions, growing new yellow petals after each burial.

CHAPTER 7

GRUP

I never did figure out exactly what made Dad come up with Grup as a nickname for Mom. To be honest, I am not sure if Mom knew why either. She never did explain it to me. I did not bother to ask her why or how Dad came up with it. I just accepted that it was funny to imagine Dad calling his wife Grup. Since I knew Mom for my forty-plus years when she was alive, I could only guess Dad would call her Grup because her mood was a conglomerate of being grumpy or up. One day, out of the blue, Mom was very grumpy with Dad when she found out he had traded a car for a motorcycle. She would tell me the story so well, it was as if I was right there with her, talking to him. "Bill, how in the heck am I going to the grocery store with four kids on that thing?" It was not long until Dad came home with a brand-new car, a 1973 pale blue Volkswagen Beetle, and Mom fell in love with it. "Wow!" She even gave it a name, Hugo. I may have asked her once what made her come up with Hugo, but I forget what she said. When I look at the name now, I remember how Mom had that car for fifteen long years, giving her four children rides to West Virginia, Connecticut, Delaware, and the grocery store; it would hug all of us tight inside and was always ready to go. Maybe that's where the name came from.

It tickles me still when I remember Mom telling me her memories of Dad calling her Grup. It was an unusual name and yet funny. I would have loved to hear and see Dad saying it. I loved the story of Dad calling Mom Grup when they were hosting a cocktail party at home where his boss was present. Dad had leaned over to Mom, whispering in her ear, "Grup, where are your shoes?" Mom was serving drinks and appetizers barefoot, and when asked about the shoes, she shrugged her shoulders at Dad and carried on with a smile. As I have no memory of Dad and Mom having fun together, I love to imagine Mom being loose and happy instead of being sad and lonely as a widow.

It made sense that Mom felt comfortable walking on the kitchen floor without shoes. For as long as I can remember, Mom swept and cleaned the kitchen floor on a daily basis, sometimes twice or three times a day when the four of us would drop our food and spill our drinks as we ate our meals. I remember walking barefoot through the kitchen many times and not once stepping on a crumb. My feet would still be clean by the time I left the kitchen. When Mom told me the story of being barefoot, her eyes lit up and her smile grew like a flower.

Mom saved Dad's eight-millimeter tapes of movies he recorded and would show them to us once in a while by using the projector. Our living room wall was the screen, and the film was silent. I imagined Mom being called Grup as Dad tried to get her to look at the camera right when she did not seem too fond of being in the spotlight. Since I can read lips, I could tell Mom was trying to be up while pleading with Dad not to film her at that moment; she said to him with a smile that almost faded into a grumpy look, "Please, Bill." I thought that scene was lovely because it was the only interaction I saw Mom having with Dad in my lifetime.

Dad had made up nicknames for the four of us little brats as well. David was called Pap pap paricho, Hannah was Khanna Anna, Emily was Boo boo badicus, and I was Mikhailovitch. I remember it well because Mom told me many, many times. She would always smile and giggle whenever she shared with me what Dad used to call us. When I was alone, Mom would tell me Dad saluted when calling out my nickname. He would click his heels together tight, stand up as tall as he could, and yell out loud, "Mikhail, Mikhail, Mikhailovitch!" To this day, I still do not know what made Dad like Russian names and doing the Russian dance, where a person drops to the floor with their legs stretched out, kicking one foot out and bringing the other in. He had someone else use his camera to record him doing the Russian dance, which, of course, everyone was laughing at because he was with his siblings and their spouses.

Dad would also film Uncle Mike when he was over at our house with his kids while Aunt Mimi and Mom were somewhere together, talking about God knows what. I remember a scene from Dad's film of Uncle Mike holding his daughter on his hip, telling her to wave goodbye to Uncle Billy. It was moments like these I was grateful for being able to read lips. However, there were a lot of moments I had difficulty understanding what was being said. When I tried reading lips at family gatherings after Dad's death, especially when the topic was about Dad, it was really hard since several people were talking at once. When two or more lips are gathered, it is chaotic for me since an average brain is only able to decipher one person talking at a time. If another person joins in the conversation, a lip-reader like me can be overwhelmingly challenged to understand what is being said because my brain tells me, "Information overload. Please abort." Naturally, I need to leave the conversation so I can regain serenity and then ante up again by looking to talk with just one person.

Since many of the deaf and hard-of-hearing people I know experience being overwhelmed when not understanding what is being said in a group of two or more people, especially at family gatherings when everyone else is not deaf and speaks without knowing sign language, it amazes me to hear many of them say they still love their families. It is as if their hearts radiate from the stars of the skies to the abyss of the oceans. Although we share the fact that it is frustrating to not be able to engage in conversations as much as we would like with family members at a gathering, they show me that looking for the positives can help relieve the feeling of self-pity. In my case, because I am a lip-reader, I am glad when I can tell everyone what was said on Dad's films, what the coach said while he talked angrily on the sidelines, or what Mom was saying as she sat in her car, driving by as I was in another car with my siblings. Usually, she just wanted us to know she would meet us at the destination because she needed to get gas first. Memories like these make me want to jump out of the car and join Mom, now that she is unseen.

In our backyard when the weather was nice, Dad filmed David, Hannah, and Emily when they were kids. David and Hannah would jump in front of each other to get the spotlight while Emily, always camera shy, stood alone quietly clapping her hands.

As the youngest of the family, I did not get to be in many of the films Dad took, probably because Dad was becoming sicker from the cancer. There is one film of Dad and me sitting next to each other on the sand at Bethany Beach in Delaware. I believe it was Dad's friend Steve who was holding the camera. I love the shot; I was happy sitting next to Dad, and he smiled at me as I turned my head away to play in the sand. My cerebral palsy was evident in that my neck was loose, my head tilting up and down as if it were about to fall off, but Dad was not bothered by it. He just sat next to me, smiling as if he was glad to be well enough to sit with his family instead of being cooped up alone, bedridden, and in pain from cancer.

CHAPTER 8

MY DAD, MY HERO

As much as it sucked being without Dad, I am beyond grateful for what he did for me in the short time he was here. Three days after I was born, Mom begged Dad to take me back to the hospital because my skin was yellow, I had stopped eating, and my eyes had rolled back into their sockets.

Mom said, "Bill, Michael is dying!"

Dad took me to the hospital, where the doctor told him I had RH incompatibility of the blood, and I needed to undergo a blood transfusion. After the doctor warned Dad that there was not a high success rate of RH babies surviving, Dad, being Catholic, arranged for a priest to come give me a baptism and last rites. Obviously, I survived, but Dad didn't. He saved me while he was dying. He is my hero. Mom said when she saw me at the hospital afterward, she almost threw up because there were tubes sticking in my legs, which were cut wide open.

Dad saved me, but Mom also rescued me from misery while I was recuperating. She said I would not smile, and my entire body was stiff. In the backyard later in the spring, Mom spent hours in the afternoon with me; she believed fresh air was therapeutic. When I did finally smile, Mom said she felt proud of herself for she was the one who got me to finally enjoy life. I loved listening to her tell me that story because she lit up with joy each time she did.

Things seemed to be looking up after I recovered. Dad got a license to fly noncommercial planes as a newfound hobby. I am proud to know he even flew the great Billy Kilmer, former quarterback of the Washington Redskins. I am not sure how they met, but it was cool to know Dad flew someone famous. He also flew his younger brothers, who adored him.

Dad grew up with eight siblings. Aunt Rose, Uncle Mike, Uncle Tony, Sam, and Dad were the first five children. They were one or two years apart in age. The last four children, Megan, Stephen, and the twins—Peter and Doug—were born about five years later, alson one or two years apart. While Dad was living with his younger brothers, he took time to build them a go-kart, and they were on top of the moon, flying fast with the wind in their hair as they zoomed downhill.

Dad did such a great job in trying to include his younger brothers on his outings, as he knew they were having a hard time at home with their parents being alcoholics. Dad's parents would be more or less intoxicated all the time. Once, Grandma was found on the floor passed out and with bruises on her face. Dad often tried to intervene. His friend Mark came over to visit one day and saw Dad knock down Grandfather and yell, "Don't you ever fucking touch her again!" I imagined Dad being Ali, standing over a knocked-out Liston.

While Grandma got sober in the early '70s, Grandfather continued to drink and eventually died of a heart attack. The subject of him became taboo, and his name was never mentioned whenever we stepped inside Grandma's home or whenever we were around her.

In the movie *Shawshank Redemption*, Red speaks of his friend Andy, who escapes from jail after being wrongly accused for murder, "I have to remind myself that some birds aren't meant to be caged. Their feathers are just too bright. And when they fly away, the part of you that knows it was a sin to lock them up does rejoice."

Dad's feathers were too bright to stay on earth when he fought cancer from ages twenty-three to thirty-two. As sad as it was to know he died so young, many of us rejoiced to see our hero finally free.

◯

CHAPTER 9

CIRCLES

I n the mornings, Mom liked to have quiet time to wake herself up. She would have a cup of black coffee and lean her elbows on the kitchen counter between the sink and oven, her favorite place. She would watch the birds through the tall windows as they pecked for food on the yard filled with weeds and dandelions, while dew blanketed the entire grounds and sparkled in the morning sunlight. Mom loved silence, especially when the four of us brats were sound asleep. Sometimes, I woke up first to go downstairs to watch cartoons on Saturday mornings, and knowing Mom liked quiet, I would turn off the volume. I did not need sound to understand why Bugs Bunny was running away from Elmer Fudd with a rifle in hand. Closed captioning, a method to create subtitles on the television screen for deaf and hard-of-hearing audiences, did not exist until 1977. It was hopeless to use sound anyway, for I could not read the cartoon characters' lips. When everyone was awake, of course, the volume would be on, and my hearing aids helped me hear the sounds of a gun being fired at Bugs Bunny and the music as he was being chased by Elmer Fudd. I am still impressed by Mel Blanc's ability to voice each of the characters; he switched from Bugs to Elmer and then Elmer to Bugs. Mom would come downstairs next while the rest of the gang slept a bit more. Instead of saying anything to me, she would tiptoe from her bedroom, down the stairs, and through the living room, patting my butt with her toes—I was always on my stomach while watching television—to let me know she was awake before she disappeared into the kitchen to sip her coffee in absolute silence.

Mom told me, "Michael, your dad would be the opposite as he loved to be loud in the mornings. Showered, dressed up, and shaved, Dad would jump into the kitchen, interrupting my moment of silence, and shout at me, 'Good morning, Grup!' "

Mom kept a wall calendar on the side of the cabinet that stood out over the oven, and she always wrote notes of what she did each day. She reminded herself to feed her plants by writing a capital *F* with a green marker on every other Wednesday. On our birthdays, Mom circled the number with a yellow marker, as if she was drawing a bright sun to highlight her joy of motherhood. When I asked her why she did not circle her own birthday, she said we were the important ones. I was always tickled to see December 25 highlighted in yellow as she wanted to celebrate Christ's birthday too. For Good Friday, Mom drew a black circle around the date to acknowledge Christ's death.

When Dad came home from a sales conference in Bermuda, he had a picture of the group of attendees in front of the hotel and drew his own circles on some of the faces with a red marker. Mom asked him what the red circles were for and Dad replied, "Those are assholes." Dad fell in love with Bermuda's weather and its palm trees.

With Dad losing the battle with cancer, his request to renew his pilot license was rejected, and his outlook on life was thick with gray skies. With the chemotherapy, radiation, and loss of his hair, Dad was not up for entertaining. When there was a neighbor who wanted to say hello, Dad immediately rushed into the house and closed the door behind him. Instead of being loud and happy in the mornings, Dad lay quietly on the sofa. He was so sick, he could barely move. There was a vomit pan on the coffee table. The four of us punks would crawl over him as if he were a football field.

Although the sofa was hideous, an awful choice of green, white, and yellow threads meshed together and a hunk of dark yellow foam sticking out through the side cushion that was torn from us jumping up and down on it, laying on it was heaven. We all felt as if our bodies could mold perfectly into the soft cushions like cats; we would sleep on it for hours. Dad loved it, too, before he went from being full of rip-roaring life to a couch prisoner holding a vomit pan. Then, the couch became his bed of woes.

As sick as he was, Dad still managed to join us, along with his friend Steve and his family, for a gathering at Bethany Beach in August 1973. It was his last summer. Steve took all his kids and the four of us with him to go crabbing to give Dad a break. I do not remember seeing Dad at the beach, but I do remember the crabbing incident. Steve was upset when he found all the crabs he caught spilled out onto the street.

We had accidentally knocked down the bucket, sending the crabs to freedom. It was short-lived, of course, as they all ended up as roadkill. Years later, when I went to interview him to collect memories of Dad, Steve told me a shocking story. When he was alone with Dad in the cottage while the rest of us were playing at the beach, he said Dad was in such terrible agony, he beat his head with a hammer so he would not feel the pain. There was blood. Steve then concluded: "That is all I have to say about that."

I am still stunned when I think about how sick Dad must have been, and yet he still managed to get out of the cottage to record his children dancing on the boardwalk. Well, most of them. I was somehow off the boardwalk, stuck in the dunes and trying to get out while being whipped by the sticky and prickly grass. Dad panned the camera from the group of my siblings, who were jumping up and down waving at him and saying, "Hi, Daddy!" to me alone, fighting with the dunes. My head bobbled and my hands flew upward with my arms pulled back; my fine motor skills were out of whack as I had not yet started physical therapy for my cerebral palsy.

Mom took me to get physical therapy for ten years to improve my fine motor skills. I could not hold a pencil or a crayon, so I was given exercises by my physical therapist to improve my grasp. I remember one of them was to pick up coins using my thumb and one finger, alternating with each finger. For example, I had to grab a dime with my thumb and my pointer. After I set the dime back on the ground, I had to pick it up again with my thumb and my middle finger. When I was done using my thumb and pinky, I would go backward, from pinky to pointer. I had to do these exercises repeatedly about ten times.

When Mom showed the film again in our living room, my cousins, siblings, Mom, Aunt Mimi, and Uncle Mike always chuckled at the beach scene. It was as if Dad wanted us to continue laughing and enjoying life. However, I admit I was not always amused. I did not want to be reminded of having cerebral palsy, which made me stick out like a sore thumb. If my siblings and cousins were to want to watch the film with me now, I would do it only because I see it is about Dad making us smile.

On January 3, 1974, Dad was at the hospital and about to close his eyes forever. He uttered his last words to Mom, "I want to go home." Each time Mom shared with me her memory of Dad before he died, she stood perplexed at the kitchen counter with the tall window behind her and said, "I still wonder what he meant when he said, 'Home.'" Now that Mom has died, I feel safe to say maybe it meant both places at once, to be home with us and in heaven, free from sickness. Every year after that, Mom circled January 3 with a black marker so she would never forget that day.

When I saw the movie *American Beauty*, I thought of Mom when Annette Bening acted as the widow whose husband was just shot and killed. She pulled down his clothes that were hanging in the closet when she realized too late that she loved him. I know Mom was not that dramatic. She simply said it was hard for her to clear out Dad's clothes and go through his paperwork. However, Mom did experience a tearjerker moment when she found an envelope addressed to her from Dad. As a surprise, he had purchased plane tickets to take Mom to Bermuda for her upcoming birthday. Her birthday was in March, which meant he probably purchased those tickets two months ahead. Mom said she sat there looking at the tickets and cried. Uncle Mike surprised Mom and Aunt Mimi with a trip to Bermuda years later for their birthday.

To be honest, as Mom and the four of us continued to live our lives without Dad, times were rough for all of us. When I looked at Mom's calendar and saw the black circle, my heart felt as if it had been socked hard by the devil, giving my soul a black eye. There was a hole in our kitchen ceiling from the time we had a leak. Dad had poked at the soaked plaster to just get a feel of it. Mom laughed each time she told me the story, especially when she got to the part where the water gushed out as Dad's finger went right through the ceiling. Instead of looking at the hole in the ceiling with a smile, I felt I was looking at the mirror and seeing the hole in my soul. As for Mom, she never once said anything about the black circle, and she just left the hole in the ceiling alone like it did not exist. However, I could see it in Mom's eyes that her soul withered into sadness. They drooped when she was feeling overwhelmed by her exhaustion after being a mother and widow for too long.

In her moments of silence, as she looked through the tall window with her elbows leaning on the kitchen counter, she brought lit cigarettes to her mouth; each time she inhaled, little specks of tobacco ignited as if her soul were angry and bitter. As a deaf person relying on lip-reading, I also need to look at facial expressions to gather what is being said. Sometimes, there is no need for words to know when a person is sad. When I think back to those moments of watching Mom staring into the backyard as if hope were lost, I want to go there and give her a hug.

CHAPTER 10
OUR FIRST CHRISTMAS WITHOUT DAD

I think it was truly remarkable of Mom to carry on with our first Christmas without Dad by arranging a Santa Claus to come over to our little house to give us presents on Christmas morning. I was a bit skeptical when he ho-ho-hoed through the back door of our kitchen instead of coming down the chimney. I also remember his stomach being flat and thinking Santa was supposed to be fat. But when he handed out the presents from his red bag, my skepticism went out the window. I am not so sure who the guy was, though he may have been our neighbor from up the street. It was really nice of him to sacrifice his own Christmas by spending it with us. Mom did a great job of making sure that instead of being miserable, we had a joyful Christmas.

Mom had every Christmas decoration up, just as if Dad were still there. The plastic stockings hung on the nails that were hammered into the hearth. The stockings were quite tacky. Of course, as a kid I did not care, for I was only excited to see what was inside. On the front of the stockings were pictures of Santa with a fat belly, which was more like how I liked to perceive him as being. On the very top of each stocking there was a white brim, as if it were fur on Santa's boot, and it showed a printed name for each of us kids. The stockings were arranged left to right from oldest to youngest—David, Hannah, Emily, then me. The back of the stocking was a clear piece of see-through plastic. David often took us to see the stockings before Mom woke up in the early morning. He showed us what we got by shining his flashlight on the clear piece of plastic as he tilted the stocking around to see what was inside. The hooks on each of our stockings were not very strong, and they ripped easily when we excitedly yanked the stockings off the nails. For the remaining Christmases we celebrated together, Mom replaced the hooks with safety pins. Each Christmas, there were new holes where the safety pins flew off when we yanked the stockings down from the hearth. The poor stockings each had a gazillion holes by the time most of us moved out.

Mom made sure each Christmas at home was special. She would give out presents from the little bit of money she could save from January to December after paying the bills from Dad's meager social security benefits. There would be a small tree, stockings, and gifts for all of us to enjoy. I remember one year when I opened my presents, I was overjoyed with my K2, a peewee-sized football. Playing football was a big part of our family, thanks to Dad's love for the Redskins. David and Hannah watched the games on Sunday, and I was very happy to follow in their footsteps. David and I both would play street football with our neighbors. One time, David's K2 was pumped with too much air, and the black rubber inside popped out of the white lace. The ball looked like it had a black hunchback.

I also received McDonald's five-dollar gift certificates, and I was more than satisfied because I loved their french fries and chocolate milkshakes. I definitely should have been more careful trying to suck up the thick shake through the plastic straw when sitting in the backseat of our moving car. The tip of the straw would always jam my palate when going over bumps. I still drank the shake even with the blood in it. The cold ice cream helped heal the cut at least.

Every year, I knew all my siblings were happy and content with their gifts as much as I was. We knew Mom scrimped and saved money all year just so we could have a Christmas. She always said we need not be greedy since Christmas was not our birthday but the birthday of our Lord, Jesus Christ. Looking back, I do not think she had to bring that to our attention. I believe we already knew what she had to go through to get us gifts, and we respected her too much to even dare be anything but grateful. We knew Mom relied on Dad's social security benefits, which was a limited amount each month. After paying rent and bills and buying food, beer, cigarettes, clothes, and shoes for her children, Mom managed to put aside a little bit of money for Christmas presents. She did not overspend, yet the credit card Mom had was never fully paid off. She said she tried to always pay the minimum, and she never missed a payment. While Mom did have Nana for support, she never dared to ask for more than what was needed. I believe Mom did a great job trying to make it on her own as a responsible head of the family and mother. Life for Mom was not about materialism but about family.

Mom had a kind landlord who knew of her situation—being a widow with four children—and he blessed her by lowering her monthly rent payment. As I look through the pictures over the years, I notice the house needed more and more TLC. The heat vents were showing cracked paint on their borders, and the walls were in need of resurfacing as the cracked lines climbed them like vines. I remember my bedroom also had cracks up and down the walls.

In the basement, each time there was heavy rain, muddy water would seep through the walls from the tiny cracks buried in the ground along the foundation. As a child, I would imagine I was a giant, crossing over muddy rivers. Mom always said she did not want to bother the landlord for repairs; she was afraid the rent would go up.

After opening our gifts and dumping everything out of the stockings, we gathered in the kitchen where Mom made us coffee cake and scrambled eggs. It was a Christmas tradition. We were all in heaven as we slowly devoured the coffee cake with our little mouths; the topping—a combination of butter, cinnamon, and brown sugar—was especially delicious.

I sometimes look at the pictures of us together as a family on Christmas mornings, sitting by the tree and opening our presents. We were all so happy and content. Even without Dad, we still managed to find happiness as long as we had each other. I miss that. I wish we were still close. However, the third Christmas without Dad ripped us all apart.

~~

CHAPTER II
A GROSS POINT

In December 1977, Mom got all of us so excited for Christmas. She kept saying over and over, "We are going to visit the cousins!" Although we were obviously visiting Uncle Mike and Aunt Mimi as well, Mom thought the visit would be more exciting for us if we knew we were going to spend time with our double-first cousins. If she said we were spending Christmas with Uncle Mike and Aunt Mimi, the excitement would not have been so great. Mom loved to see her four children happy and figured out the word "cousins" would make our eyes sparkle with delight. Mom exclaimed with glee, "We are going to have two Christmases to celebrate—one at home and then the second one with the cousins!"

When Dad was alive, he always seemed to be the host, as he loved entertaining guests. It was not a surprise to see pictures of my siblings and me having birthday parties with our cousins at our house. They lived close by until Dad died. At that time, Uncle Mike was called by his boss to relocate. Uncle Mike still managed to visit us when he was in town on his way to the farm, his getaway home in West Virginia. Aunt Mimi and Mom just had to see each other to relieve themselves of the "twin separation anxiety" thing. Mom, my siblings, and I were always invited to join Aunt Mimi and Uncle Mike at the farm for a week in the summers. Of course, we also had the tradition of seeing the cousins at the farm for our annual Thanksgiving get-together.

When we were all little, we cousins would spend a lot of time together. We played in the creek nearby and took walks through the property, seeing mountain ranges and deer. There was a barn full of hay, and we would all go to the loft to jump down into the pile of it.

I remember my oldest cousin, John, would help me work on my speech as I had trouble with enunciation, especially with the letter *s* because I cannot hear it. Sometimes I say "sh" when I really want to say "s." John loved to watch television, so he had me work on saying the word "Sony." When I tried to say the word—I do not remember if I said it correctly then—he cheered nonetheless. He had everyone hold hands, all seven of us—John, Meg, Paul, David, Hannah, Emily, and me—and we jumped into the hay pile as if to cheer me on for saying the word. It did not matter if I actually said "Shony." To them, my effort was good enough, and that was fine with me. When we were apart, we would all be pen pals, and I remember getting scratch-and-sniff stickers from my cousins. My favorite was the slice of pizza sticker. When I scratched it, the aroma of pizza came alive. It was really neat!

Mom made me super excited when she said we were going to travel by plane to visit the cousins. For big trips like that, I could only imagine Mom using her favorite blue credit card with the Choice Visa logo on it. She always said she used the card for the big things and paid a little bit each month. She had interest, but with payments every month, her credit was outstanding. The banks loved her too.

When we all arrived at the airport in Detroit, flying from National Airport in DC, we found a chauffeur waiting for us. Uncle Mike had arranged for a limousine to pick us up. I never asked why he did that for us, but I could imagine he wanted us to feel privileged somehow, as he knew we were struggling financially with Mom being a widow. He probably just wanted to pump up our spirits. It was so fun riding in a limousine for the first time, playing with the automatic locks. I also jumped from seat to seat in the back since they faced each other. Seat belt laws were not yet in force. Mom had a picture taken of us standing together in front of the limousine. The picture was amusing because we were about to ride in a fancy car while wearing mismatched clothes.

All of our clothes were secondhand, worn, and a bit oversize. My Redskins jacket and most of my clothes were handed to me from our tall neighbors up the street. I was short and barely saw my fingers poking out of my sleeves. I wondered if Mom wanted me to have big sizes so she would not have to worry about shopping for a while. I had to wear a pair of pants on top of another layer of pants just so I could fit in them because I was so skinny. We looked like we were the *Beverly Hillbillies*. Mom used to dress up when Dad was alive. She wore nice dresses, and her hair was neatly trimmed. Without Dad, Mom seemed to stop caring about her looks.

She had very little time to groom when she had four kids to take care of without any outside help.

When Mom was revving up our little spirits by telling us we were going to see the cousins for Christmas, I knew she was really excited for herself since she was going to get a break from us kids. We would all be busy playing with the cousins, so she would have time to catch up with Aunt Mimi. It would be like when they were together before they both got married, talking up a storm in their own twin language that no one else could understand. I felt good about that because it was the only time I was like everyone else.

The chauffeur drove us to Grosse Pointe, Michigan, a wealthy area where the Fords lived, but I did not know that at the time. The cousins lived in a mansion, and there was real, white snow on the ground. The outside of their house was decorated with white Christmas lights. No one in the rich neighborhood dared to have tacky, colored bulbs flashing on display. I jokingly said if these people knew Mom had her tree full of them at home, Aunt Mimi and Uncle Mike would have been shunned for just knowing her.

I was floored when we went inside because I had never seen two sets of staircases in the foyer, which was so large we could have fit our little house in it. When I saw their Christmas tree in the living room, I was amazed by how beautiful it was. The decorations on it were impeccable, especially with the little white lights blinking all around it. Our whole property—the house, garage, and driveway— could have fit inside the living room, it was so humongous. All of this made me get my hopes up too high, for I imagined getting more than a few presents on Christmas morning.

Before I knew it, my cousins were running downstairs to the living room to open the presents that awaited them. My siblings and I quickly followed with excitement, both for them and ourselves. Under the beautiful tree, there were gorgeously wrapped presents. The gifts reached the ends of the walls, and it seemed as though the floor was full of them. My siblings and I opened ours after waiting for the cousins to open theirs first. I am not sure what my siblings got, but I remember I was intrigued with what looked to be a tiny, neon-orange, plastic trash can with neon green goo inside. On the label, it read Slime. I was fascinated with how cold it was as I squeezed it with my hands, seeing the goo popping out of my closed fingers. I looked to see what my siblings were up to and saw them looking at our cousins with facial expressions of polite envy. Their eyes were sad while they tried to smile as our cousins continued to open their presents, tossing ripped wrapping paper in the air. I quickly found myself growing sad and wearing a polite smile too, as there was nothing left to do but painfully watch our cousins continue to go through the entire floor of unopened presents.

I then decided to check on Mom to see how she was doing, and I felt terrible when I saw her crying as she stood next to Aunt Mimi near the kitchen, their arms stretching into the kitchen door to keep their cigarette smoke contained. When she saw me looking at her, Mom quickly ducked back into the kitchen, as if she did not want anyone to know she was upset. Out of all the memories Mom and I would share in our little kitchen over the years, the Christmas in Grosse Pointe was never mentioned. I never thought about asking her what exactly had happened that made her upset. Since I will never know for certain what made Mom shed tears that Christmas morning, I can only guess that she, too, was sad that her four children had to sit and watch their wealthy cousins open many presents.

I, of course, wished we had a lot of presents to open like our cousins did. I somehow assumed that was a benefit of having a father, to be financially well-off and have a grand Christmas. The Christmas at the cousins' house was life making a gross point to me, that it sucked not having a dad. For the first time, I saw a yin-yang of how different our families were. They were rich, and we were poor. They had a father, which made their family complete. We were fatherless, and that made us look like an incomplete jigsaw puzzle, Dad being the missing piece.

I know Uncle Mike and Aunt Mimi did not intend to put any one of us down, especially Mom. I doubt very much Aunt Mimi deliberately invited Mom for Christmas to make her cry and say to her, "Hey, Annie, my husband is alive and I am rich. Your husband is six feet under, and you are poor." It was Aunt Mimi who hugged Mom in her kitchen and gave her comfort when she cried. It never dawned on me then that perhaps Mom was also upset to see her two disabled sons next to Aunt Mimi's two boys without any disabilities, just two good-looking, normal guys. Lucky bastards.

Mom said to me later, "Michael, I wish you and David were like Mimi's boys."

Yes, it does hurt sometimes when I think about that. However, if I put myself in her moccasins in that moment, I understand where she was coming from, which helps me to not take it personally. Mom was still vulnerable as a widow then, for it had been less than three years since Dad died when we went to Grosse Point. She may have been grieving, but she did not realize until she saw for herself what was missing in her life, a life with Dad. She probably asked God silent questions in her heart such as "How could you do this to me? Why does Mimi get the good apple and mine is rotten? What did I do to deserve being a low-income widow with four little children who are fatherless? What did I do to cause my mother to dislike me? It was not my fault that my own father died. It was not my fault that Bill got cancer after we were just married. What did I do to deserve two sons with disabilities? Why do I have to look across the room and see two normal boys who came out of my identical twin's womb? Isn't Mimi from the same embryo as me? Aren't we supposed to share the good, ripe apple?"

I could be wrong about the questions she might have asked herself, for I never sat down with her to discuss her thoughts about that Christmas morning. I let her be. I did the same for years when I saw her cry every Christmas after the one in Grosse Point. I just watched her sob quietly to herself as she stared through the kitchen window while smoking a cigarette. Maybe she was thinking, "Michael, get a job and leave me alone."

~~

CHAPTER 12

LIKE MOTHER, LIKE SON

Days before Mom died, she looked into my eyes and said in a weak voice while smiling, "I see you in me." I did not know what she meant by that at the time. I did not ask her what she was talking about.

Now, as I look back on what she said to me, I can say to her, "I think I know what you meant."

While it was a fact that we both lost our fathers when we were four years old, anything I say after is mostly my perspective of how similar we were. We were both suffering from depression, addiction, and poor dieting. On a brighter note, we both shared a liking for nature, God, going out to the local diner, watching movies, and eating cereal.

With Mom standing alone in the kitchen and smoking her cigarette, I could sense she was suffering from depression. Her face was tilted down, her eyes staring at the kitchen counter instead of looking straight out the open window with sunlight shining through, which was one of the sights that made her fall in love with the kitchen in the first place when Dad showed her the house. I knew in my heart there was something wrong with her.

Perhaps it was all the smoking, drinking, and lack of nourishment that contributed to her depression. If I were to give a house plant nothing but beer, blow smoke at it, and deprive it of water or nutrients, the plant would not survive the first few weeks. Mom had been drinking and smoking since she was sixteen years old and stopped just a few weeks before she died at sixty-four, so it was not surprising to learn she had lung cancer and that it spread to her brain.

Maybe Mom suffered from a mental ailment, which could be genetic. She once told me about her great Aunt Rosa being sent to a psychiatric institution due to a mental illness. I did not ask Mom to tell me more about what happened to Aunt Rosa. I just sat there in the kitchen and listened to her talk. She did not volunteer to tell me all the details either.

When it was just Mom and me in her house after I reached my twenties, I noticed she was alone most of the time. She did not have friends to visit. Nana would invite her over for dinner from time to time, and when Aunt Mimi was in town, Mom would get together with her. When Nana and her friends got together on Thursdays to play bridge, Nana would invite Mom to join them. Other than that, Mom spent most of her later years standing alone in front of the closed blinds, staring down at the counter with a cigarette in her hand. When Mom said to me, "I like being alone," the sadness in her eyes could not convince me her words were entirely true.

I could joke that my being there until I was in my thirties had something to do with her sadness, but honestly, the memory of her being alone and sad because Nana and Aunt Mimi already passed away makes me still feel sad for her. I hated that I couldn't do anything to revive her spirits. I would have loved it if Mom had been like that woman I often saw standing in front of a beach cottage in Bethany when I was on my way to swim at the beach. That woman was lively, and her children and grandchildren were always sitting in the yard and having a barbecue. It was painful to realize that Mom had not had a great life like that lady in the front yard had. I could be so wrong about the woman being truly happy, for we do not know what goes on behind closed doors. However, I liked to imagine Mom having the time of her life with her family instead of being alone in her kitchen with the blinds pulled down during a beautiful morning sunrise.

***

As a depressed college dropout, I usually woke up in the late afternoon, and I kept my blinds down in my bedroom, which used to be Mom and Dad's before Dad died. One day, I found a note on the nightstand from my sister Emily. I do not remember exactly what she said, but she encouraged me to seek help. Whereas Mom was able to function as a part-time teacher's aide even when she seemed depressed, I was depressed and completely dysfunctional. I had quit two different colleges, and I spent too much time sleeping in my bed.

I honestly believe depression is a progressive illness that gets worse over time if it is not treated. I saw it happen to both Mom and me. While Mom went from being perky and upbeat to sad and somber, I also went from being positive to feeling shitty about my life. When I was five years old, I ran up to a low tree branch in my neighbor's yard and jumped as high as I could, touching the branch and feeling tall, mighty, and victorious. Years later, in seventh grade, I was suicidal. At first, I thought it was because I was rejected by a girl I liked yet barely knew, but it is now obvious to me that the girl was just a symptom of my depression.

I was depressed but did not know it. I did not see the bigger picture I had hidden in my subconscious: Dad was dead, David was abusive, and I disliked who I had become: a freak with hearing aids and cerebral palsy. It was not normal for a twelve-year-old kid to swallow a bottle of migraine medication just because he asked a girl to go out with him when they barely knew each other.

At fifteen, I wanted to get to know my high-school peers better, so I went to a party since I was not showing up for classes as much as I should have been. I had been struggling with depression for years, and I liked the idea of faking sick and being allowed to stay home. Of course, that ended up backfiring on me since I ended up missing too much school as I got older. I had no idea I would have a drinking problem because of that one night. I often took sips of Mom's beer with and without her permission, but I had never lost control. At the party, where I knew no one and my sister Hannah had dropped me off, I immediately went to the keg and poured myself a cup of beer. The next thing I knew, I was zigzagging in the backyard and then waking up on a couch with a girl who was weaving her fingers through my hair. I thought I was in love, which was crazy since I did not know her at all. I did not even know her name. She may have gone to the same school as me, but I was not sure. I remember asking her to meet me after school the following Monday, but she never showed. I felt pathetic because I actually believed I had a new girlfriend. I had been so excited to finally meet a woman who cared for me. I mean, why else would she spend time weaving her fingers through my hair? Again, pathetic. To this day, I still do not know who the mystery girl was. Sometimes, I wonder if the girl was actually a boy. Oh well. I guess I will never know.

At some point, I remember being carried to my bedroom by a good Samaritan who knew my sister. The next time I opened my eyes, I saw Mom laughing at me. I was not hungover, but she obviously knew what I had been up to. We never did have a conversation about what happened at the party. I sometimes wonder if she was laughing because she thought it was funny to know her son had a great time at a party, or so she hoped.

After that, I hung out with my buddies I had met at the local shopping center, and we smoked cigarettes we had stolen from our mothers. We drank beers on weekends in shacks, behind school buildings, and at random parties. During my first year of college, I met my first girlfriend, Abigail. There was an icebreaker during orientation in the form of a dance. I had already seen Abigail earlier on campus, and when I walked by, she gave me a nice smile. I felt lovestruck. I was nervous but also determined as I walked up to her on the dance floor. Long story short, I asked for a dance, she accepted, and we dated for about four years. While being in love for the first time, I was also doing well academically. I thought I was happy.

However, during my second year of college, my mood started to slip downhill like a pebble that was set loose after an earthquake. I still had to choose a major and a career, but I had never thought about what I really wanted to do. Although I ended up deciding to be a social worker because I thought I was a nice guy, I knew I was lost. I did not know it at the time that social work was not for me. I just acted like it was because I believed it was college or bust. My two sisters went to college. Mom, Aunt Mimi, and Nana all went to college. My double-first cousins went to college. I thought the next steps after high school were to go to college, get a degree, and work until retirement. In the end, though, social work was not for me. It would have been better if I had stayed at my job at the gas station. I had no other ambitions, so getting paid to pump gas probably would have worked for me.

Instead of telling anyone about my doubts and anxiety, I suppressed my fears and turned to drinking beer. In my second year of college, I began hanging out with the guys and gals who liked to party. The dorms were filled with superficial laughter as we were all pretty much scared of what we were facing: our future. The toxic air was a mixture of fake laughs and cigarette smoke as we attempted to drown our fears with beer.

I knew I was in trouble when, one night, I sat in front of my studies and could not open my textbook. The outlook of my future was dim as I was not sure what I wanted to do with my life, and I was overwhelmed with fear that the best solution I could come up with was suicide. I then made an appointment with the psychiatrist on campus. During our first session together, he handed me a pencil and asked me to draw any picture I wanted and bring it back for our next appointment. I drew a picture of a big house with many windows, and I thought the doctor would be impressed with my artistic talent. I liked to draw when I was younger, so I thought I was rather good at it. The psychiatrist sat across from me at our next appointment with a serious but calm look on his face. After handing me back the paper, he said to me, "I think you are depressed." I was floored, for I had never heard anyone say that to me before. I knew I felt depressed, but I thought I was doing a good job at fooling everyone else into thinking I was fine. The psychiatrist, John, put me on an antidepressant, but it did not do me much good. My visits with John were short, and I decided to take a leave of absence for a while. As I continued to drink, smoke pot, and party, I stopped taking my antidepressant because I had no interest in improving my mental health. It was not a conscious decision to stop the meds and continue wallowing in self-pity. It just happened. It was like I was on autopilot, heading straight to self-destruction.

Abigail saw I had become distant from her and her friends and that I had been hanging out with the wrong crowd. She wanted me to tell her what was going on. We were hanging out at the apartment she was living in because it was near her internship. She was going to graduate soon and was ready to work in the real world. Since the day I met her, she had always known that she wanted to be a phlebotomist, and she often teased me by holding my arm out and pretending to draw blood. Anyway, the mood was dark while we sat in her kitchen. Eventually, she just asked me straight out, "What is wrong with you?" I could not give her an answer. I honestly did not know what was *really* wrong with me. Instead, I responded with nervous laughter, hoping she would stop digging into something I wanted to keep buried. I was not spiritually or mentally ready to dictate what was the matter with me.

One morning on campus, I had not gone to sleep for I had been out drinking and doing drugs all night. I was on my way to work or class—I cannot remember which—but with my mind fogged with drugs, I knew there was no way I would be able to focus. Instead, I surrendered to sitting on a bench, and all I could do was watch students walk back and forth to their classes, the library, or the dorms. I just watched life happen, and the pain of not being a part of it was too great for me to accept. I eventually had to remove myself from the action of watching people living productively and returned to my dorm to sleep.

My first memory of feeling detached from college life was during the fall of my second year. I sat in the restaurant with Abigail and her friends at an Asian Deaf Club dinner. I felt as though I was drifting out of my seat while I sat there and looked at the table full of people who were smiling, laughing, and talking with each other. My heart became sore as I could not bring myself to smile, laugh, or strike up a conversation. I became numb; it was as if my spirit went AWOL. I knew I was frowning and some people were taking notice, so instead of creating a scene, I quietly got up and walked outside for some fresh air. As I stood outside, leaning my back against a pole, smoking a cigarette, and staring into the parking lot in a daze, Abigail and some of her friends came out to show their support and see what was wrong with me. I still could not give an answer. I do not remember what happened after that moment, but I was in trouble and did not know how to get myself out of it.

I knew smoking was not good for me. It was definitely not good for Mom; I knew that even as a kid. I had tried to hide Mom's cigarettes so she would be healthy, but she scolded me and told me to never touch her cigarettes again. Abigail tried to tell me I had a problem and needed to address it, but like Mom, I did not want to be bothered. I was stubborn and didn't want to stop my self-destruction. It was weird considering I had wanted Mom to stop smoking and drinking.

After dating for four years, Abigail eventually moved on and fell in love with another man. She called to tell me her news. I was not too shocked since I had stopped talking to her for about six months before she called. I was too addicted to pot and beer, and I did not bother thinking about other people. Honestly, I did not even deserve a call from her. I treated her badly all because I was scared of not knowing what to do with my life. Her parents hated me, and they had a good reason to. I was an asshole. I sometimes called them when I was drunk and high and told them what I really thought of them. Needless to say, the words I spoke during those calls were not kind. It was actually ironic that I would call her parents like that considering I barely called Abigail to see how she was doing while we dated. When she and I did get together, it was because I would just show up out of the blue while I visited our college campus for the sake of getting drunk and high. I might as well have been wearing a sign on my back that said, "Beware: ridiculous college dropout on the loose." After Abigail and I hung up, I was heartbroken, but I did not cry. I knew Abigail deserved better.

By that time, I had transferred to another college closer to home. With not many credits earned over the four years in my previous college due to withdrawing from too many courses and leaving campus for two different semesters, I enrolled as a sophomore at Gallaudet University, a four-year liberal arts college for the deaf in Washington, DC. At the end of the fall semester, I received a 0.0 GPA. Before I left my dorm to go home again, I cried in the dark and asked God to help me. It was then that I received the breakup call from Abigail. I was so miserable and depressed, I decided to invite over some strangers I had met at a party off campus. It was in a neighborhood you would not like to walk through late at night: some dangerous guys lived there. As we were about to smoke weed in my dorm, I suddenly realized my life was unbelievably screwed up. I was hanging out at a college that was waiting to kiss me goodbye, and I was about to smoke a bowl with dudes I did not even know. They probably were not even students. It was in that moment that I realized I desperately needed help. I decided to enter a twelve-step program and give sobriety a try. During the meetings, I heard stories of women who recovered and felt like better moms, and I wished the same for Mom.

I once asked her, "Mom, do you want to give sobriety a try?"

She smiled and said, "No. I am okay with my life the way it is."

Even with sobriety, I still struggled with depression and did not fully understand it. I thought maybe I was not doing something right because other sober people seemed to be so happy, and I was still miserable. I wanted Mom to have a better life, but I felt I had no right to help her since I was struggling to bring my own head above water. A drowning man cannot save another drowning person, even if she is your mother.

My good moments—when I felt like my head finally broke through the water's surface—were usually during my twelve-step meetings. In those moments, I often looked at the two sets of window blinds that were pulled down on the wall behind the speaker. On one set of blinds was the inscription of the twelve steps and on the other, the twelve traditions—guidance on how to achieve sobriety both individually and in groups. I would smile at the blinds as I remembered my past days of sleeping my life away in the dark with the blinds closed while the sunlight was shining brightly on the other side. It felt good to let myself be embraced by the light since I had grown sick and tired of turning my back on the light … and love. I had no idea how much hate was stored in my heart and how much I appreciated the feeling of opening my hands and heart to peace. I wanted that for Mom, but one of the hardest things about life is that sometimes we cannot do anything but watch someone we love slowly drift away and die.

I believe poor dieting was one of the symptoms of my and Mom's ongoing battles with depression. When my siblings and I were growing up, Mom made sure we ate three meals daily. Even as a kid, I noticed Mom was not eating much while she served our meals. I figured she wanted to serve us first and stand prepared with a sponge in hand just in case we spilled something. If Mom did eat, it would be the leftovers on our plates. After we finished eating, she would use the sponge to wipe off our mouths and hands before we left the table. She wanted to make sure we did not stain the doors, walls, furniture, and television. I remember Mom smiling and saying to me as she wiped my face, hands, and fingers clean with her sponge, "Okay, Mikey, all clean. You may go now."

When my siblings and I started working part-time jobs after school, we missed many of the dinners Mom prepared. She was frustrated with us for not being home after she spent her time cooking. She had to watch as the food she prepared got cold and then dispose of it. One day, she decided to put her foot down and yelled, "Kitchen's closed!" Mom stopped serving meals for us every night after that. Instead, she would only serve us holiday meals whenever we were home for Thanksgiving or Christmas.

When my sisters and brother moved out, Mom and I began having just one meal a day. In the evenings, Mom would eat cheese with crackers along with beer and cigarettes. As a side dish, she had a bowl of milk and shredded wheat and would eat it later in the night before bed after drinking a few more beers. Likewise, as I did not eat all day, I would go to a local diner at night for a late dinner, usually around nine. I filled my stomach with French toast, scrapple, two eggs—sunny-side up, of course—and toast to dip into the yolk.

Sometimes, Mom would let me eat a bowl of cereal for breakfast, lunch, and dinner, but she would get upset when she noticed the milk was suddenly low. I felt bad, but I did not do anything about it. I just expected Mom would get more. I did not realize it then how much of a brat I was. I am sure it was killing Mom to hold her tongue when all she wanted to do was speak her mind: "My house is closed! Go find your own! Buy milk and I will come over there and chug most of it just so you can see how I feel!" Honestly, I think there were times when she was trying to throw subtle hints at me to get the hell out of her house—I was still living with her at thirty-something—but I was too obtuse to see them. When I wanted to cook a meal, she said, "No, you may not touch my pans. You will ruin them." When I wanted to do my own laundry, she said, "No, you will break the washing machine."

***

While Mom and I shared signs of depression, addiction, and bad dieting, we also shared healthier interests like mowing the grass, avoiding gossip, and watching movies.

Mom mowed the lawn every summer after Dad died. I never did ask Mom if Dad used to mow the lawn. It just did not occur to me. No wonder I sucked at being a therapist. I was not good at asking clients questions, especially hard or painful ones. One of my clients was a student who was deaf and mentally disabled. My job was to sit with him in his classroom and help him stay seated so he could pay attention to the teacher. As much as I loved the boy—he also had cerebral palsy, and we both had the same name—he was beyond my help. He would constantly get up from his seat while the teacher was talking and run around the classroom. Sometimes, he would grab the teacher's hair and not let go. The lesson would then be put on hold as we waited for the school counselor to intervene. I kept telling my supervisor that the student needed one-on-one instruction and physical therapy so he could learn with less stimulation. My supervisor did not acknowledge my concerns and kept telling me to just sit with him.

I did such a bad job at counseling that I would try to make fun of myself just to help me feel better. I would say something about how I did a better job at selecting the melted brie lobster omelet than offering therapy. But I digress.

As a child, I enjoyed watching Mom going up and down the yard with the mower puttering loud like a helicopter without propellers. For whatever reason, the idea of mowing a yard fascinated me so much that when I was in my early teens, my first job was cutting grass in the neighborhood. My first client was our neighbor next door. Mom would tell me how thrilled she was to see me mow as close to the fence as I could get so she did not have to fuss about how carelessly the neighbor mowed away from the fence, forcing the tall grass from her side to lean into Mom's yard. With Mom potentially being obsessive-compulsive, the leaning grass trespassing her yard drove her crazy. I found it funny to see Mom clench her fist at the neighbor, not only because her dog would howl all day and night but also because of her grass tilting into Mom's yard. I did not tell my mom or my neighbor that I mowed so close to the wired fence that I was cutting the wires apart. I figured no one would notice since the bruised wires were tucked under the grass. I was relieved when no one said anything to me about it. In fact, I was proud of myself for a job well done. Every time I finished mowing my neighbor's yard, she would hand me fifteen dollars and smile, telling me I did good.

**

If someone asked me what Mom's biggest pet peeve was, I would say it was that she couldn't stand gossip. She refused to participate in the neighbors' circle outside on the street.

Mom said something to me once about gossip that struck a chord in my heart forever: "Michael, what if I was in the group, participating in the gossip about someone who was not present? I believe the person in the group who is not present the next meeting will be the victim of backstabbing."

I would look at the circle of adults from my bedroom window upstairs, shaking my head at them for proving Mom right. They should have been ashamed of themselves. Though who am I to judge? I wasn't actually sure what they were saying; I couldn't lip read from my bedroom!

My wife, Maura, likes talking about people at her workplace who do not do their jobs. Sometimes, I dismiss myself from listening because I believe she is gossiping, and I do not like to gossip. Maura often tells me she is not gossiping, just venting her feelings. I then tell her to try not to bring her work problems home because home is a place to feel at ease.

I do not share Maura's idea of venting because I tend to keep my thoughts to myself. For Maura to get me to express myself, she has to get in my face—nicely, of course—and demand to know what I'm thinking about.

I always try to smile when I respond, "Nothing."

I remember having a similar conversation with Mom in the kitchen one night when I tried asking her how she was doing. She looked at me with a smile, tilted her head away from one of her magazines so I could read her lips, and replied, "Fine." She then politely turned her head away from me, her eyes returning to her magazine.

Mom did have a number of friends she could talk to whenever she wanted, but she chose to isolate herself and seemed content in doing so. Growing up with her, I thought that was just who Mom was, someone who liked to be alone, be available for family, and dwell in quiet. I like all of those things, so I had assumed Mom liked them too.

Maura usually wants me to go out with her and the kids to socialize with other parents or people in general. I often decline, telling her that as a stay-at-home dad, I need a break from kids. Sometimes, when she leaves with the kids, I am relieved to be alone at first, but later, as I get more and more lonely, I feel regret for not going out with them. Most of the time, however, I feel content with my decision to stay home so I can watch television without sacrificing it to my kids as they often want to watch Disney Plus when I want to watch an R-rated movie.

Mom and I liked watching movies. One of the best movies we saw together was *Groundhog Day*. We loved it! I liked it a lot because Bill Murray's father-figure character was funny and had a good-paying job. Of course, I did not consciously tell myself, "I must see this film because I have a void in my heart for not having a father, and Bill Murray will come to the rescue." I probably was not the only one who had that void. Maybe there were folks who did not have mothers growing up, and they appreciated watching Andi MacDowell portray the soon-to-be wife of the wacky weatherman.

When the movie *Good Will Hunting* was playing in the theaters, Mom went to see it alone. I felt so bad and asked her, "Mom, why didn't you ask me to come with you?"

Mom smiled her usual smile and said, "I did not want to bother you." I was studying to pass my classes at Gallaudet University for the second time around, but I would have jumped at the chance to see the movie with Mom so she would not have had to sit in the theater all by herself, surrounded by people she did not know. Mom then told me, "Michael, you will love that movie. You have to see it."

I rented it so I could follow the movie with closed captions, and she was right. I did love it. I loved seeing the relationship between the therapist and client so much, I wished I had a therapist, or even a dad, like him, even though I knew he was just an actor. I wonder if Mom liked the movie because of the way Robin Williams's character was a kind of father figure for Will. Since she also did not have a father growing up, Mom could probably imagine how good it felt for Will to have someone care about him in a way only a father can. Years later, when I learned Robin Williams died by suicide, I was dumbfounded. I would never have guessed he suffered from depression.

Mom and I were suffering from our own depression, and maybe we both hoped that the end of our road would be good like Will's as he drove across the country to give himself a better future by making peace with his tormented past. I daresay Mom essentially died by suicide because her depression became too great, especially when her friends and family passed away. Mom must have thought it was too much for her to go on alone, but I wish I could have made her realize she was not alone. She still had her four children and seven grandchildren who loved her. Likewise for Robin Williams, he was not alone, for he had friends, an ex-wife, and children who loved him. I hope I do not ever put my own family through such heart-wrenching pain.

As I look back on the last few years of Mom's life, I can now see that I do not have to live my life the same way she did. I did not realize how much I had molded my life to be like hers. If she really had given up, I do not want to feel as though I should too. The hole in the ceiling, the missing knife in the kitchen that David, my brother, had used in his attempt to kill her, the cigarette stains on the kitchen walls, and the damaged plaster on her bedroom wall from David stabbing at it were like ghosts dwelling in Mom's heart in order to reinforce her beliefs that she did not deserve to have a good life. God knows I am trying, for Mom's sake, to allow myself to believe that I deserve a better outcome—for my family, the two grandchildren she never met. I want to go to heaven and know I did not die by my own hand. I do not look down on those who choose to take their lives. They were sad and wanted to be free of their pain. I just hope I can find the strength to overcome my depression and look back on my journey with a smile.

CHAPTER 13

A MOTHER'S JOB IS NEVER DONE

Life was not always a rainstorm in our family unit. Mom did an excellent job in trying to keep all of us busy and happy. For instance, she loved driving us around in Hugo. The name seemed to suit the car just fine—it was cute enough to hug, and it was always on the go, even with the rusted floor pans and holes that showed me how fast the car went over the gravel.

From 1973 to 1988, Mom took us to many places. She drove us to our piano lessons and to each of our recreational sports after school. We also went on trips to Bethany Beach in the summers, and of course, Mom drove the windy roads for our Thanksgiving visits with our cousins in West Virginia.

One night, Mom took me, Aunt Mimi, and Aunt Mimi's youngest son, Paul, for a ride. I was maybe nine years old and had to pee, but because we were in the mountains with no place to stop, I was too afraid to ask Mom to pull over.

I tried my best to hold it in. The back seat where Paul and I sat was made of slippery leather, but I still hoped my urine would soak into the seat, should such an event occur. Unfortunately, as I could no longer contain the rapids, the warm pee traveled as the car continued winding roughly with the narrow mountain roads, and it managed to greet Paul in a rather warm but unfriendly way. Paul immediately leaped out of his seat and shouted something. I did not know what he was saying for it was too dark to read his lips. I could just sense the emotion was not pleasant. Of course, I hated that I had to be the unlucky one who had to pee at the worst possible time. Oh well. It could have been worse.

At night, sometimes Mom would drive us to Shakey's, a good, old-fashioned, family pizza restaurant that used to be on Rockville Pike near Congressional Plaza. I loved Shakey's. When you walked through the front door, there was a long glass wall on the left side and a bench underneath so kids could stand and watch the pizza chefs toss dough, insert it into one of the many oven slots, and keep the fire going. Mom left us there while she went to order the pizza and get a table for us to sit down together. She patiently waited at the table alone, knowing we would all come to her sooner or later to sit down and have dinner. I do not mean to be a sourpuss, but I wonder how hard it must have been for Mom to sit there alone while knowing, at the same time, there were families all around her with two parents talking with their little ones.

One night on the way to Shakey's, a flash flood thunderstorm halted drivers, who were blinded by the quick downpour on their windshields. Mom was frantic but tried to stay calm by saying a little prayer out loud as the four of us peeked through the windows with amazement at just how much rain was coming down from the skies above. Suddenly, the rain stopped, and the sun peeked back at us through the dark clouds with a present in her pocket: a rainbow she then threw across the sky to let us know all was well. Mom took the rainbow to be a sign from God, letting us know He was always there to help the fatherless and widowed. I was so happy that night, for I collected a lot of quarters from the jukebox as I jiggled the coin return button, and *whoosh*, a handful of coins flushed out of the dispenser. As I look back on that night, I felt like I was a leprechaun finding gold at the end of the rainbow.

Some nights, Mom took us to the mall to go shopping, usually at Kinney Shoes. It was the place to go back in the late 1970s to get shoes. Montgomery Mall used to be a smoking-permitted building with reddish-brown floor tiles that made the entire mall dark and hideous. Mom would park Hugo in front of Sears; she liked entering the mall through there. Sometimes, she would buy us clothes that were cheap brands like Toughskins pants. Kinney's sold Adidas look-alike sneakers with stripes on the side. Mom would tell me one of her favorite memories was when we were at the mall and I was playing with the escalator buttons since they were not covered back then. I pushed the red one, and an old lady fell off. I assumed the lady was okay because Mom never mentioned her being injured. No news was good news, eh?

Mom would smile and chuckle, looking at me with her beautiful blue eyes, before saying, "Michael, you then walked up to me and asked me, 'Are you my muvva?' You had not yet gone to speech therapy, so you had trouble saying words, especially 'mother.' You would call me 'muvva' instead. I felt embarrassed that you would not know your own mother, so I leaned toward your face and said, 'Yes, I am your ever-loving muvva.' "

Mom took David and me to Easter Seals for speech therapy. I still had trouble with enunciating letters I could not hear like *s*. I had to learn to put my tongue behind my front two teeth, resting the tip against the bottom of the two teeth, and slowly blow air through. For words with *ch* as a prefix, I had to raise the tip of my tongue and rest it against the very top of my two front teeth to enunciate the letter *t* and then immediately transition to combine it with *sh*. To this day, I sometimes find it hard to enunciate every word clearly, so it is no wonder I'd rather say "shit" than "church."

I also went to Easter Seals for ten years of physical therapy to improve my fine motor skills and audiological support for my hearing aids. The audiology department is also where I went to receive speech therapy. I loved my physical therapist because she let me drive an electric toy car that I would often crash into the walls and water fountains. I also loved my audiologist for she was beautiful and kind.

Because David and I have disabilities, Mom attended four Individual Education Plan meetings a year for over twenty years at Montgomery County Public Schools, where we both attended. It was required by law for her to be present to approve the teaching plans for both curriculum and accommodations given. As for Hannah and Emily, Mom wanted them to have the same privilege she had growing up and attend private Catholic school. So when they were in sixth grade, the girls went to St. Jane de Chantal. Then they moved to an all-girl's Catholic high school at Holy Cross

Academy. I remember watching Mom work hard at nights, filling out financial aid forms twice a year for the girls so they could get the quality education she had at Stone Ridge.

All the while, Mom was at home, washing our clothes, cleaning the floors, vacuuming the rug, cooking us dinner, making us individual school lunches per each of our requests, and even mowing the yard with the same lawn mower Dad used. The mower was a Craftsman, and as much as the thing was falling apart—shoe strings were tied to keep the handle from falling off—Mom would still use it to cut the grass. Our neighbor from across the street was always glad to help keep it alive, thanks to his natural-born talent with repairing and building engines from scratch, as long as Mom provided him with a batch of brownies she made from scratch. Mom said his mother told her he refused to share the brownies with anyone; he kept them hidden in his room.

In addition to all of that, she also had to deal with us troublesome brats. Whenever the four of us dared sneak into Mom's closet to get a clean shirt out of the wash pile, where she kept the clothes hidden from the cigarette smoke downstairs in the kitchen, we would get an earful. We were choosy in what we wanted to wear, and most of the time, our favorites were in the wash. We could not wait for Mom to put them away. I tried to get away with it by being as neat as possible, but it was hard for me to take my shirt out without accidentally dropping other clothes. I think maybe my cerebral palsy made the crime messy; perhaps, I was just terrible at being super neat like Mom. She shouted through the walls, "Who went through the wash pile?"

In the kitchen during dinner, whenever we spilled milk— well, I was mostly the culprit—we all watched the milk travel quickly down the walls and onto the floor, knowing we were about to be kicked out in a second. On cue, Mom would yell at us, "Everyone out! Kitchen is closed!" Sometimes, we had not yet finished our meals and were still hungry. We all popped our little heads through the kitchen door a few minutes later and asked Mom if we could come in. She'd yell at us, "No!" We then slowly backed away from the door opening, as if we were turtles bringing our heads back inside our shells. We then waited for Mom to clean up the milk and sit down for a minute before finally telling us we could come back in.

God, I miss her.

CHAPTER 14

MARK

After Dad died, his childhood friend Mark would send a Christmas card every year to Mom and she would read it to us after Christmas dinner in our kitchen. She stood up with her back leaning against the counter, facing my siblings and me as we sat on our bums. It felt like we were at school, and Mom was the storyteller while we were her students.

I tried to read Mom's lips, but my mind was distracted on what else was inside Mark's Christmas card—five, crisp one-hundred-dollar bills. Mark instructed that the money was only for Mom. However, instead of keeping the money all to herself, Mom always shared it equally, handing each of us a one-hundred-dollar bill every year. My eyes grew exceptionally big each time one was delivered to me. The last bill was put away neatly with the card; Mom probably wanted to read it again when we went to sleep.

Mom knew David and I wanted the money right away, but she pretended every time that she did not know what was in the card. She would slowly open it in front of us after we sat down, impatiently waiting for her to read the card out loud. It was excruciating for me to sit on the stool and wait for Mom to finish reading before dispersing the cash. I did not care too much for the tearjerker moment when Mom and my two sisters cried because Mark was a true novelist at heart, especially when talking about how much he loved Dad.

If there was any man who could have replaced Dad, it would have been Mark. All of us loved him. He always remembered our birthdays and would send us birthday cards with cash. And when Mom was with Mark when he visited us after Dad died, I saw how happy she looked being next to a man. At five years old, I was too young to ask myself if I wanted Mark to be my dad. But I knew Dad was not with us, and when I saw Mark, I felt happy too. One year, Mark went with us as a family to West Virginia to visit Uncle Mike, Aunt Mimi, and the cousins for a week. I thought the relationship between Mom and Mark was getting serious, especially on his last night with us when he gave Mom a smooch on the lips before driving off. Although Mark was not married, he did have a girlfriend at home in California whom he married years later.

When I came to my senses as an adult, I realized I actually did want Mark to be our dad. I was between college and finding a job, and I went to visit Mark a few times. My first visit to Mark's house was in 1998 after I had graduated college and earned my degree. I had a job interview in San

Luis Obispo, California, farther south from his home, which was in the Bay Area (near San Francisco).

The job was to work with the deaf population, selling a wireless device called WyndTell. It was one of the first handheld devices made before smartphones took over. I thought I would be a good salesperson for the company because Dad was a salesman, and I was a deaf person selling a deaf product to deaf customers. It was *deaf*initely a great idea, right? No. I sucked at selling. I had zero motivation to win the customers' wallets for such a device, and I hated being pretentious just for the sake of earning a dollar. Dad and I might have looked alike, but we were different in other respects.

While I was in California, I met Mark's mother. He was living with her at the time. Maude and I clicked as instant friends. We had never met before, but she remembered my dad from when she used to live in Bethesda. Mom and Maude never met at all. Mom never did make a visit to Mark and Maude's house, but she did talk with Maude on the phone a lot. Mark said he could not believe his mother got dressed up, put lipstick on, and had a glass of wine with me in their backyard when we were having salmon on the grill. Mark said that for a while before my visit, Maude had been down in the dumps. Again, I never pried or asked why. I just accepted his word. He thought the sight of his mother being cheerful with me was a miracle. Later that year, Maude died. She was ninety-three.

Two years later, I traveled across the country with Faye, a lady friend I met in college. When I learned she was going alone, I volunteered to join her. I always liked her as a friend, but I thought our road trip might bring us closer so we could try dating. I was being crazy and selfish. She was still tormented from the breakup with her fiancé and was returning home to her family as a result. Nevertheless, we had a good time before we got to her parents' house.

At some point, her dad asked me, "So are you going to relocate here to California?"

I smiled politely and said, "Sure," but my heart was not sure. And he knew it.

I had no plan to get a job anytime soon. I was a hopeless romantic. Everyone could see it but me. Faye's friends welcomed us for a get-together, and they immediately clicked, laughing and having a good time, especially the guy friend of hers whose name I do not remember. I felt sore and depressed as my expectations to be a couple with Faye sank in that moment. I tried to boost my self-esteem by telling them we should rent a really good movie, *Good Will Hunting*. Well, the movie flopped because they had no interest in watching a film that was sad. Tough crowd. Faye was not interested in me and neither were her friends. I had to get out of there. I needed to go to a twelve-step meeting just to chill out and remember my purpose in life: stay sober and help others. It was better than going to a bar and saying to the bartender, "Feel sorry for me as you pour me another drink."

I got on the phone, using a TTY, an old teletype device for the deaf and hard-of-hearing. I called a relay service to have an operator make the call for me and to relay back and forth what the receiver and I were saying. The receiver made it clear he had no patience for sob stories while I was telling him mine about feeling like a fool. He said, "I don't care what your story is! Go to this meeting, at this address, at this time. Goodbye!" I did not remember what was said or what I said at the meeting, but I do remember feeling better afterward. I just needed a safe place so I could breathe and realize my expectations of winning over Faye were ludicrous. I was ready to move on.

After the meeting, Faye dropped me off at Mark's house. It was then I met Mark's girlfriend, Rosie. She was now living with Mark. I guess when Maude was alive, she had forbidden Rosie and Mark to live together before marriage. I am not sure. Again, it is not in my interest to explore what was going on in someone else's life. I just knew I was feeling uncomfortable. Maude was not alive anymore, and I missed her. I also felt odd seeing Rosie with Mark for the first time. The image seemed to have shattered my hope that maybe one day Mom would marry Mark. However, I think I needed to see them together so I could process it and finally accept that Mark and Mom were never meant to be a couple. I dared myself not to say a word about what I was thinking. I just acted as if nothing was wrong. I really wanted to be a good guest.

But I was uncomfortable with Mark dating Rosie. I was also angry at Mark for not keeping Dad's promise to look after Mom after he died. I did not like how he had raised our hopes every time he came to visit Mom and me. Whenever he took us out for dinner, I could see how happy Mom was to see and spend time with him. They could have been such a wonderful couple. I had hoped that Mark would one day come live with us, marry Mom, and we would be a complete and happy family again. Why not? Aunt Mimi should not always be the lucky twin.

I was not aware of how upset I was at Mark and Rosie being a happy couple until I made a disrespectful joke about

Rosie, asking Mark, "Do you want to swap wives?" The joke was more of a slip of the tongue. It was spontaneous, and it made no sense. I was feeling awkward, and therefore I was unclear with what I really wanted to say, which was, "Yo, Mom should have been the wife, not you! Hey, now that we are on the topic: Mark, did you have sex with my mom while you visited us with no intention of ever staying with her?" I did not ever make such a comment, though.

Thankfully, Rosie just groaned while Mark and Brian, an old friend of theirs who was paying them a visit, chuckled lightly. I realize now that what I really wanted to say to her was, "Rosie, you took Mom's place!"

As I think about why I said that, it makes sense that I was mad that Rosie won Mark, not Mom. I never dared to make another bad joke with Rosie. I decided it was better for me to not try to have a conversation with her except to say a polite hello whenever I spoke with Mark over the phone.

It was hard for me to fully accept that Mark and Mom weren't going to be together. There was a time when Mark gave Mom a necklace, and I saw it as a token of love. It was a delicate, gold chain with a capital *A* for Annie. Mark had bought it for Mom several years after Dad died. Through the years, Mom would take the necklace to the jewelry store to have it mended after it broke. She was working as a part-time teacher's aide at a daycare center, and the tots would grab her necklace, ripping it apart. I assumed it was accidental. My siblings and I knew how much the necklace meant to Mom. But today, I know now that the necklace was a token of friendship, especially since I had seen Mom hugging Mark and Rosie at my wedding.

***

After Mom died, I thought Mark would come to her funeral. But being older and so far away, Mark felt it would be better for him to stay home. He would have had to come all this way just to sit down with his broken hip on a hardwood church pew for a few minutes and then go all the way home the next day. Regardless, I think it was good closure to see Mom's friendship with Mark being taken with her in spirit since we decided to bury Mom wearing the necklace. Knowing Mom, she would not have had it any other way. Whether Mark came to the funeral or not, they were friends forever.

CHAPTER 15

OVERCAST

I sometimes love it when the sky is gray with an overcast of clouds when I am at the beach, looking at the ocean from the boardwalk in Bethany. I like the cool air and the drizzling of rain, for I know there will be a pool of dolphins traveling across the horizon soon. I just have to wait to be amused. However, at our little house on Greenlawn Drive, there was a different kind of overcast that darkened our spirits for over three years. It was during the time when David was being severely bullied in high school.

David had become an easy target to be picked on since he was skinny, short, and mentally disabled. His back was also deformed, and his ears stuck out. The students who were angry and in pain themselves felt at ease knowing they could displace their negativity onto David, who was harmless, before other people picked on them. I think the cycle of bullying starts not just at school but also in the home for some people. When David walked through the hallways, kids would flick his ears, causing them to be red and sore. In the bathroom, where there were no teachers to watch, David's head would be dunked into toilets. Mom said she had no idea David was getting bullied at school because he did not tell her until years after he graduated. She said to me, "I cannot believe David would still go to school every day on his bike, knowing that he was going to be tortured."

I often think about David pointing to the sky when he was about ten and I was about six. Mom stood with us in the backyard, and the three of us were looking up at a small plane flying over our little house. David pointed at it and said, "Look, that's Dad saying hello. " I liked his nice gesture, as if he was trying to make us all believe our lives were okay as long as Dad was looking after us as our guardian angel.

As I look back, I can only imagine he was heartbroken to be without Dad because he knew him much better than I did. His stock of memories are real-life interactions with Dad since he was seven when Dad died. I had just turned four, so my memories of him consist of only fleeting moments. I am not always sure if they even really happened. I remember seeing Dad walking through the kitchen in his underwear. I am not surprised if that did happen; I have done that a lot of times in front of my kids and wife. I also have a memory of when Dad was sleeping on his bed. I reached for his hand, which was hanging over the side. He grabbed mine for a second, and then he let go. Although this memory may be something I imagined, I like to cherish it as if it were real.

After Dad died, I pretended to be dead at the school playground, as if I was unconsciously engaging in self-directed psychodrama. After the teacher picked me up to bring me inside the school, I woke up and wiggled like crazy, magically reviving myself. I wanted to bring Dad back from death so I could be with him again. Children are impacted by death more than we think. For David, it must have been truly devastating. When he was being bullied, he probably wanted Dad to come back even more than the rest of us so Dad could protect him, cradle him in his arms like he did when David was born, and tell him everything would be all right. Since David was mentally disabled, I can somewhat understand how Dad's death and his own horror of being bullied were two contributions that led him to be angry and confused, displacing his frustration onto us.

It is still unclear when David actually started getting bullied. He started being physically abusive toward me when I was about seven, three years after Dad died. One Sunday morning, I was happy to be home from church. The minute I stepped out of Hugo and onto the driveway, David whacked his elbow right into my nose. I remember the pain throbbing in my nose and radiating all over my head as if my inner spirit was thrown against a rock. I cried like a baby, watching the blood drip onto the gravel. When I talk about that moment, I try using humor to make myself feel better. As a U2 fan, I sometimes joke about the incident being related to their song "Bloody Sunday." Most of the time, I do not think about it. Suppressing the bad memories helps me move on.

Unfortunately, David became increasingly violent as he grew into his teens. He was the tallest, strongest person in our house—the only place he did not feel powerless. It was as if David had a breakdown from being constantly bullied. His attacks on us were terrifying because they were unpredictable, as if he had become a boogeyman, quietly sneaking up on us and then giving us a horrible fright.

When I was eight years old, David and I shared a bedroom. He quietly and gently led me to our window. Like a flash of lightning, he suddenly shoved my entire arm directly at the glass. My wrist went through the glass and was sliced open. Mom was downstairs with a neighbor, having coffee and a casual chat, and I, being terrified of the dripping blood, waved my arm as I ran down the stairs and stuck it in Mom's face. My neighbor was horrified at the sight of my bloody cut. Her eyes bulged, and she quickly excused herself, leaving the room and exiting out the front door. She never came back for another visit.

Mom took me to the hospital, where I had to get five stitches. When I saw my old scar above the new one, I noticed it was still the champion as it had needed eight stitches. That old scar was not from David, but a neighbor's cat. I'd been too young to understand why it was not a good idea to pull the cat's tail with full force. After I'd done that, it clawed my arm before running away.

There was another incident with David when I was a bit older, maybe twelve or thirteen. I was standing in the kitchen and talking with Mom when David suddenly came through the kitchen door and shoved me from behind. I lost my balance and fell into three stools that stood underneath the kitchen nook, knocking them down. My mouth was open as I smashed it against the stool's wooden leg, and my two front teeth were broken as a result. And yeah, I cried like a baby as I sat on Mom's lap. Now, I almost wish I would have thought to thank David for making me look like a tough hockey player, but I did not have the wit back then to make such a remark. There were more incidents like that. David did a lot of scary things to me and my sisters, but it was Mom who got the worst scare of all.

Mom tried to get help from counseling, neighbors, and God on Sundays to find a miracle to tame David's angry spirit. She had David join the Cub Scouts, hoping it would help him be at ease with his peers, who seemed to be nicer than those at school. In the garage, Mom made David a woodshop, where he could channel his frustrations in a healthier manner by building things and pounding on wood instead of us. Even though Mom tried to help, David was still fuming with anger, and she was powerless to stop it. David went further downhill when he found refuge in alcohol as a freshman in high school. His anger turned more violent with a drink in his hand. Even though it was especially bad for Mom, she let David stay with her after he graduated from high school.

However, in August 1985, two months after David's high school graduation, he came home drunk and attempted to murder Mom in her sleep. He walked into our house and grabbed a chef knife from the kitchen cutlery that was hanging on the wall above Mom's calendar. After Mom miraculously escaped, she managed to call the police, and they arrested him. For two years, David was placed in a psychiatric hospital. Out of the goodness of her heart, Mom visited David there at least once a month during his stay and supported him with apartment housing afterward.

Mom had the right to cut ties with him after his eighteenth birthday, and I never asked her why she continued to support him. I assumed she feared David could not live independently because of his borderline mental disabilities.

It had to have been a hard decision for Mom, I imagine, for the resources available—such as housing for those with mental disabilities—were and are scarce. Most of the housing is suited for people who are clearly disabled and declared completely dependent. That was not David. Mom was at a loss to find David a group home where he would be cared for by social workers and case managers. Unfortunately, with Mom not wanting him to live with her ever again, she went to endless trouble to place him in apartments and, eventually, a condo, hoping that would have him settled for good. However, with a drink in hand, David ended up losing apartments and had to foreclose on the condo Mom had helped him purchase. She had given him the down payment after receiving an inheritance from Nana. As of now, David is still in the vicious cycle of alcoholism, where he cannot or will not put down the drink.

I still talk with David via texting and recently, due to the coronavirus, we occasionally talk on Zoom with my two other sisters. I love David just like Dad and Mom did. They held him in their arms as their first child. My siblings and I are trying our best to support David, for I know it pleases our parents, especially Mom, to see how we are still in contact with him. David, however, is an alcoholic. Alcoholism is an ugly disease, and it is sad to watch David drown himself, just like Mom did for years, when our hands are right there to help. Powerlessness is hard. All I can do is pray and be there for him.

CHAPTER 16

GRACE

I knew I did not belong in college. I had no idea what to major in and a habit of assuming what I know is true without checking the facts, which often led me to shoot myself in the foot. It was no different when I enrolled in the National Technical Institute for the Deaf (NTID) in Rochester, New York. I thought it would be awesome to ski on weekends since I knew how cold it could get in Rochester in the winter. What I did *not* know until I got there was that there were no mountains! It was flat all around. The closest mountain was three hours away, and I did not have a car! Pretty dumb, right? I should have stayed home, where I had a job at the gas station. Mom would have been happier with me having a job as long as I was not worrying her to death. David was not the only one on Mom's worry list. I just did not realize it until she was dying.

Well, when I was stumbling through classes, feeling lost and not knowing what I wanted to do with my life, I decided to act in two NTID performances. I mainly played the sidekick, and it certainly gave the audiences a good laugh. I was written up in the NTID magazine for stealing the show in *Great Expectations*.

I recall one night when Mom told the story of me being on stage when I was five years old, a year after Dad died. We had gone to a magic show, and I don't know what made me raise my hand as high as I could when the magician asked for volunteers. I am not even sure if he chose me, but I went up anyway. As I stood next to the magician, Mom said everyone laughed so hard because it was the first time many people had seen a kid with cerebral palsy wobbling back and forth on stage without knowing his zipper was down. Mom told me she cried from laughing so hard. So, during a weekend in my second year in college, I invited my drinking pals to come watch me do a stand-up act at a bar in downtown Rochester. Mom supported my dream of being a stand-up comedian and wanted me to succeed. She knew I liked the stage and that getting paid for being funny was not a bad thing.

It was better than trying to kill myself. I had tried to do that twice, once at home when I was in seventh grade and later in college. I just did not realize how much Dad's death and David's abuse—in addition to my self-esteem being battered by cerebral palsy—were affecting me. I did not really want to die, I just did not want to feel so bad inside. In both situations, I swallowed a full bottle of aspirin. The first time, I was in seventh grade, and I asked a girl to be my girlfriend over the phone. I liked her because she was nice to me at school, and we would hang out at the end of the day waiting for the bus to come. I would talk with her and make her laugh. When she said no to me, I felt suddenly depressed and went to the medicine cabinet. I told Mom later what I had done. After my confession, mom told me she came into my room the following night while I was asleep and wept. Nothing happened to me physically. I was fine and just went about my day after I woke up.

I did not tell her about the second attempt. I did tell my ex-girlfriend, and she came with me to the emergency room. There, I drank liquid charcoal and vomited black lava. I was supposed to be in my dorm, studying for an exam and *not* puking my guts out from a suicide attempt. Prior to this attempt, I sat down at my desk and stared at my textbook to do my homework. I did not open it. I froze with fear as I realized for the first time I was lost in my world. I did not know what I was going to do with my life, and I felt scared. I did not know how to express myself to anyone. I suppressed my feelings and tried to force myself to do my homework, but instead I cried.

While I struggled with untreated depression, I continued to smoke and drink. One night, I was driving my ex-girlfriend's parents' car. They hated me, so it really was not a good idea for me to get high and drunk behind the wheel, but I did it anyway. I was chased by a sheriff after he saw me buy beer at the local gas station and get in the car after one o'clock in the morning.

My depression affected every aspect of my life— particularly how I functioned on the job as a social worker as well as a comedian. I often quit jobs because I did not like them. I just found myself applying for deaf social-work jobs because they were easy to get since the turnover is usually high, and the desired requirements for most of the jobs were to be deaf and know sign language. At night, I went to comedy clubs and crossed my fingers, hoping that maybe I would get noticed. Sometimes, I did well onstage and rocked the house. The feeling I got from the audience loving my presence was exhilarating. Other times, more often than I care to admit, I bombed. The feeling of standing on the stage with an audience as quiet as a deer stunned by headlights was beyond awful. I traveled all the way from Maryland or Maine to New York City to be noticed so I could ride a limousine to fame, not to be walking off the stage with dead silence. I came up with a self-deprecating joke: "I need to return to physical therapy to learn how to hold on to a job."

I wanted to be able to tell Mom, "Guess what? Your prayers are answered! I have a job!"

Of course, in my mind I could hear Mom saying, "Don't blow it!"

Well, it seemed like God had plans for me when I met my wife at a deaf Catholic church. The moment I laid eyes on Maura, I thought she was beautiful, especially since she was the only woman with black hair; the rest of the women were old and had gray or white hair. After church, I went up to Maura and introduced myself. I felt like a happy dog with my tongue hanging out and my hearing aids sticking up like dog ears. Unfortunately, she was not interested in pursuing anything with me because she had just broken up with her boyfriend. However, one year later, I happened to run into her again in downtown DC. This time, she smiled and invited me for a cup of coffee. Another year later, we went off to get married.

I believe God brought Maura and me together so our wedding and reception could also be used as Mom's farewell party; she died from lung cancer about six months after we wed. Several of her and Dad's friends and family members attended the wedding. Aunt Mimi did not attend, because she had died a few years earlier. I am just so glad everyone else was able to come witness our holy matrimony and be with Mom; for many, this was their last time seeing Annie Mather.

Maura's friend Alice, who is a fantastic photographer, took a great picture of Mom sitting in her pew as she looked up at the altar and watched Maura and me exchange vows in sign language. Alice, who is also deaf, captured a side of Mom that looked completely different from when she was tired, pale, and fragile from being sick. The camera revealed a miraculous change in Mom's demeanor. The sun was shining on her, her rosy cheeks coming alive, and her eyes swimming like the glistening Caribbean. Now to me, that is what Mom was all about—grace.

~

CHAPTER 17
TIME TO COME HOME

Before she passed, Mom decided to move out of our little house in Bethesda. She relocated to be closer to Bethany Beach, as if she wanted to reunite with Aunt Mimi, Nana, and Granny so they could be the four little women again. Mom said to me, "I miss them, so being at the beach might help me feel close with them again."

I found out later that I had not helped her transition go so well at her new home. I broke Mom's heart when I visited her at the condo. It was January 2007, two months before she died. I was living in Pennsylvania with Maura in an apartment, and I had recently quit my therapist job—another job that just did not go well for me. I thought it was good timing, or a blessing in disguise, because Mom was in need of help. She had fallen and cracked her ribs while sleepwalking, and I just wanted to be there for her. I thought I was being a good son.

When I got to Mom's condo, I thought I'd cheer her up with a movie we both liked, a comedy called *My Cousin Vinny*. I popped in the movie and opened a new pint of Ben & Jerry's chocolate-chip cookie dough ice cream. When I looked over at Mom to make sure she was comfortable, I was sad to see her crying. "What's wrong, Mom?"

"Michael, what are you doing? Why are you here?"

"I am here because you need help."

"Michael, you need to be home with your wife and working. I am so worried, and I am scared for you."

Mom continued to cry. I stopped the movie and put away the ice cream and just sat next to Mom, not knowing what to say. I felt absolutely horrible. I realized it was the first time she had ever expressed that I was breaking her heart.

I had quit jobs and gotten fired before, and Mom always let me live with her without saying a word. But there I was, newly married—Maura was kind enough to let me stay with Mom—and Mom did not comprehend that I was just there to help her, that I was not running away from marriage or life. Mom thought my behavior had not changed and that worried her.

I had believed she did not mind me being with her all those years. In fact, I thought she thought it was funny to tell people her son was a typical Irish bachelor who had no plans to leave his mother at age thirty-five. I thought wrong. My behavior had hurt Mom; she just never said a word about it until she was on her deathbed. I did not want to cause any more distress in her last days. I did not want to cause her any more misery, period. She deserved better than that.

Then it all happened so fast.

Mom ended up bedridden, or sofa ridden. She eventually could not move from the lumpy sofa that came with the condo. Maura soon joined me in helping Mom. We handwashed the lumpy cushions after the hospice nurses moved Mom to the toilet to finish relieving herself. Mom's legs were bony with little flesh. She suffered incredible weight loss from not eating since the night she had her last supper: a french fry.

At the end of February 2007, Mom seemed to not mind the lumps on the couch. She fell into a deep sleep after her first dosage of morphine. By this time, David, Hannah, Emily, and I were together saying goodbye. On March 1, the four of us were visiting Mom, who was still asleep on the couch, when she suddenly let out a cough. To my surprise, Emily quickly leaned forward and said, "Mom?" I had thought Emily did not care overmuch about Mom because she did not often make herself available. For example, when Mom was in the hospital after her mastectomy, Emily never showed. Maybe when she saw Mom cough, Emily felt guilty for never being there for her. Maybe she wanted Mom to feel better so Emily would have a chance to make up for the things she had done wrong. But I cannot say for sure, and it is not my business to know what goes on between two adults. I do know that I loved Mom and wanted to stand up for her when I thought someone was treating her badly.

So it was nice to see Emily so concerned for Mom. We all were as we leaned forward with her, hoping Mom would wake up. It was disappointing to see Mom return to her deep sleep and not make another sound. I could tell she was still breathing since her chest was slowly moving up and down. Sometimes, I think it is funny to imagine Mom coughing and, realizing her four brats were by her side, quickly returning to being comatose because she was done being a mother.

On March 3, 2007, with Mom still lying on the stupid, lumpy couch, her face became too difficult to look at. The eyes were no longer bright blue like the Caribbean. They were unfamiliar and beastly, glazed with yellow-brown pus, detoxing from nicotine withdrawal. Her eyebrows were thickened and wet from the ooze spilling over. All four of us were begging Mom to please go because we could not stand to see her like this anymore.

The morning of March 4, Mom was still breathing. David stayed with her while Hannah, Emily, and I were out. Emily went with her husband somewhere, and Hannah and I went to Wawa to get coffee. On the way there, Hannah's phone rang. It was the hospice nurse. She hung up and made a quick U-turn back to Mom's cottage. She told me that Mom's breathing was shallow; she was going to die any minute. Hannah called Emily and we all met together at Mom's. As Emily stepped inside, Mom decided it was time to go. She left on a beautiful, sunny morning.

It was weird waiting in the condo with a dead body lying on a lumpy couch for the funeral men to come and retrieve what used to be Mom. It was weirder as I suddenly found myself alone when the two funeral men came inside. My siblings and wife had gone inside the guest bedroom, closing the door behind them. I decided to stay with the men and gave them a hand. The three of us picked up Mom from the couch and inserted her into a body bag. One of the men suggested I zip the bag closed, as it may provide good closure. I don't know why, but that irritated me. I did not want a stranger to tell me how I should tell my own mother goodbye. It would have been better if he had just quietly let me help them. That would have been good closure. I watched the zipper slowly close up the bag over Mom's face, and it was then I said goodbye in my heart. I walked outside with the two men, one holding the door open and the other holding one end of Mom. When the hatch of the hearse closed on Mom's body, I stood in the middle of the street alone, watching the hearse drive away until it disappeared.

On the way home, Maura and I took Route 1 north. On the right side, there was the ocean; the bay was on the left. As it was evening, the sun was setting on the bayside in order to go to sleep under the western horizon. Stretching across the sky was one of the most spectacular sunsets I had ever seen. The colors of pink, red, orange, blue, and purple were splashed across the sky, with the bright yellow, red, and orange sun giving a kiss to the east as it journeyed to the west.

Right then and there, I knew Mom was wide awake. It was as if she had blossomed into a beautiful butterfly, fluttering happily into the sunset, away from me. With that thought, I just knew Mom was smiling her usual smile and saying, "Thank God."

CPSIA information can be obtained
at www.ICGtesting.com
Printed in the USA
LVHW111534300921
699106LV00001B/115